GREAT
MARKETING
IDEAS

FROM LEADING COMPANIES
AROUND THE WORLD

Jim Blythe

Marshall Cavendish
Business

Copyright © 2009 Jim Blythe

First published in 2009 by

Marshall Cavendish Editions
An imprint of Marshall Cavendish International
1 New Industrial Road, Singapore 536196

Other Marshall Cavendish offices: Marshall Cavendish Ltd. 5th Floor, 32–38 Saffron Hill, London RC1N 8FH, UK • Marshall Cavendish Corporation. 99 White Plains Road, Tarrytown NY 10591-9001, USA • Marshall Cavendish International (Thailand) Co Ltd. 253 Asoke, 12th Flr, Sukhumvit 21 Road, Klongtoey Nua, Wattana, Bangkok 10110, Thailand • Marshall Cavendish (Malaysia) Sdn Bhd, Times Subang, Lot 46, Subang Hi-Tech Industrial Park, Batu Tiga, 40000 Shah Alam, Selangor Darul Ehsan, Malaysia

Marshall Cavendish is a trademark of Times Publishing Limited

A CIP record for this book is available from the British Library

ISBN 978-0-462-09942-2

Designed by Robert Jones
Project managed by Cambridge Publishing Management Ltd

Printed in Singapore by Fabulous Printers Pte Ltd

CONTENTS

INTRODUCTION

IF YOU PICKED this book up, you are probably looking for some new ideas. You might be a marketer yourself, you might be an entrepreneur or small business person, or you might just want to be able to drop in a few good ideas at the next meeting. This book will help with any of those aims.

Marketing is, above everything else, about creating profitable exchanges. The exchanges should be profitable for both parties—fair trade always makes both parties better off, otherwise why would people trade at all? What we are aiming to do is offer products (which includes services, of course) that don't come back, to customers who do come back. One of the basic concepts of marketing is customer centrality—in any question involving marketing, we always start with looking at what the customer needs. This does not, of course, mean that we are some kind of altruistic, charitable organization: we don't GIVE the customer what he or she needs, we SELL the customer what he or she needs. Note that we define needs pretty broadly, too—if a woman needs chocolate, or a man needs a beer, we are there to ensure that they do not have to wait long. Most of the ideas in this book offer you ways of improving the exchange process, by encouraging more of it or by making the exchanges more profitable.

Marketing goes further than this, though. Marketing is also concerned with creating a working environment, with managing the exchange between employer and employee for maximum gain for both parties. In service industries, employees are a major component of what people are buying—the chef and waiters in a restaurant, the stylists in a hair salon, the instructors in a flying school. Some of the ideas in the book are about internal marketing: keeping employees on board and motivated is perhaps the most important way you have of developing competitive edge.

This is not a marketing textbook. There are plenty of those around, and if you are a marketer you will have read plenty of them. There is very little theory in here—only one or two examples when they help to illustrate the reasoning behind some of the ideas. The aim of the book is to offer you a set of "snapshot" ideas for marketing. The ideas all come from real companies. Some are big, some are small, some are service companies, some are physical-product companies. In some cases, you will be able to lift the idea completely from the book and adopt it for your own business: in other cases you might be able to adapt the idea. In still other cases, the idea might illustrate how a creative approach can help you, and perhaps it will spark off a few ideas of your own.

The ideas often came from the companies' own websites or from published sources, and in other cases came from direct experience of dealing with the companies themselves. If you keep your eyes open, you will see examples of slick marketing all around you—a creative approach is all it takes to be a winner yourself.

Ultimately, good marketing is about being creative. Successful companies are the ones that develop their own unique selling proposition (the USP) that marks them out as different from their competitors. The USP might be almost anything—an improved level of service can make all the difference to a firm selling a product such as cement, which is essentially the same whoever sells it. At the same time, a retailer with an exclusive range of physical products can create a strong competitive advantage over another retailer who is equally attentive to customers and has just as nice a store. Copying ideas directly is usually not a good idea—but adapting them from a different industry can be extremely powerful.

A common mistake many firms make is to try to please everybody. For all but the largest firms this is impossible—and even very big firms tend to do it by splitting themselves into various subdivisions and sub-brands. You can't therefore adopt all the ideas in this book: you will have to be a bit selective, because many of the ideas will not apply to your industry or your individual circumstances. For small to medium-sized firms, specialization is the way forward—but specialize in customers, not products. Customers give you money, products cost you money: stay focused on customer need!

Ultimately, without customers there is no business. This is true of staff, stock, and premises too, of course, but they are all a lot easier to get than customers—after all, everybody else is out there trying to get the customers' hard-earned money off them. I hope this book will give you some ideas for getting more customers, keeping them for longer, and selling more to them.

Jim Blythe

1 GIVE THE PRODUCT AWAY

GIVING THE PRODUCT away might seem crazy—but in some cases it is the only way to establish it in a new market. When a product is revolutionary, few people want to be the first to try it, so asking them for money up front often simply creates a barrier. In some cases, this is just something we have to live with, but if owning the product means that the customer will have to buy repeatedly, giving away something that creates a dependency is good business.

There are many examples in practice of products that are sold cheap, with the company making its money on the peripherals. Spare parts for cars are an example—the cars are sold relatively cheaply, but genuine spares are expensive, because that is how the manufacturer makes money. There is no reason at all to be wedded to the idea that every product that leaves the factory gates has to have a price tag on it, and many companies have succeeded admirably by giving products away.

The idea

When King C. Gillette invented the safety razor he was working as a salesperson for a bottle-cap manufacturer. He conceived the idea for a disposable razor when his cut-throat razor got too old to be resharpened: he fairly easily developed a way of making the blades and the razors to hold them (the first blades were made from clock springs) but economies of scale meant that the blades could only be profitable if he could manufacture them in their millions. He needed a quick way of getting men to switch over from cut-throat to disposable razors, so he decided to give the product away.

Gillette gave away thousands of razors, complete with blades, knowing that few men would go back to using a cut-throat razor once they had experienced the safety razor. Within a few days they would need to buy new blades, so Gillette had created an instant market, limited only by his capacity to give away more razors.

In time, once the product was established in the market and the first users (the innovators) had started telling their friends about the product, Gillette was able to start charging for the razors themselves. However, the razors were always sold at close to, or even below, the manufacturing cost—the company makes its money on selling the blades, which cost almost nothing to produce and which can be sold for a premium price.

In time, other shaving systems came along (plastic disposables, for example) that superseded Gillette's idea, but the basic marketing idea remains and is still used to this day.

In practice

- Identify products that carry a long-term commitment to buying peripherals, spares, or other consumables.

- Decide your target market—there is no point giving out freebies to all and sundry if they aren't going to follow through and buy your product later.

- Make sure you have good intellectual property rights (patents, etc.) so that nobody can enter the market with knock-off consumables that work with your giveaway product.

MAKE IT FUN

MAKING YOUR MARKETING fun for customers is what makes them tell other people about you. This is the basis of viral marketing—the word of mouth that ultimately generates more business than all the advertising campaigns put together. Humor is good, but something that encourages customers to pass on messages to friends, business colleagues, family, and indeed anyone else will result in improved brand equity and increased awareness of what your company is all about.

The message need not be too serious, either, or indeed be an overt marketing plug. Just passing the brand name along, and having it associated with something entertaining and fun, is quite sufficient. Your other marketing promotions will fill in the gaps, and anyway no single promotion will ever cover all the communication you want it to—the best you can hope for is that one communication will sensitize the customers to receiving a later one.

The idea

Radisson Hotels serve a predominantly business clientele. Business travelers typically spend a great deal of time in their rooms: they tend to use the time to catch up with work rather than go out sightseeing or to entertainment venues, since this allows them to spend more time with their families.

Radisson hit on the idea of supplying each room with a plastic duck to play with in the bath. The duck came with a note saying that the guest was welcome to keep the duck, perhaps to take home for his or her children: if the guest preferred, however, the duck could be mailed anywhere in the world in its own special crate, with a message from the guest. Mailing the duck incurred a nominal charge that could be added to the guest's final bill: the charge was, in fact, more than enough to cover the costs of the duck, the crate, and the postage, but in luxury hotel terms it was small.

The result of this was that hundreds of thousands of Radisson ducks were soon finding their way across the world. Children, girlfriends, husbands, wives, friends, work colleagues, bosses, and business associates began receiving the ducks, which no doubt raised a smile. The effect was to raise the profile of Radisson, but more importantly it changed the brand personality—the stuffy, formal image of the typical business hotel chain was modified, showing that even a top-class hotel has a sense of fun. The shift in perception contributed to a growth in Radisson's weekend family trade, and made business travelers more likely to stay.

In practice

- Do something that is fun.

- Ensure that it is as easy as possible for someone to tell others about the experience.

- Try to have something tangible attached to the experience so that there is a permanent reminder of the event.

- Be careful that the message (in this case, "We like to have fun") does not detract from the rest of the brand image.

3 GET DECISION-MAKERS TOGETHER

In most companies, especially larger ones, there is no single decision-maker. Even the top boss needs to consult other people in the management team. Salespeople often try to get all the decision-makers together for a presentation, but in practice this is usually impossible: senior people have busy diaries, and are certainly not going to inconvenience themselves for the purpose of being sold to. Key-account salespeople therefore have to talk to the various decision-makers individually, and hope that when they do talk to each other (usually without the salesperson being present) they will agree to go ahead and buy.

In many cases, people who do the everyday buying work within tight parameters that they cannot contravene. In order to change anything, they need permission from someone else, who will usually pass the buck back again. Creative marketing can break this deadlock. Using the right type of promotion can ensure that the key decision-makers talk to each other: if it's done really well, they think the meeting was their own idea.

The idea

When the first long-life low-energy light bulbs appeared they cost around ten times the price of a tungsten-filament bulb. Although they used only one-fifth of the energy of a traditional bulb, this was not enough to make them cost-effective, but they last 50 times longer, which is a major advantage. The problem for marketers lay in persuading people that this was worth while.

Osram, Britain's biggest light bulb manufacturer, reasoned that the new bulbs would benefit businesses much more than consumers.

The reason is not the energy savings: it is the maintenance cost of replacing bulbs. Paying someone to change light bulbs in an office building is expensive—but nothing like as expensive as changing them in a warehouse or factory, where the bulbs might be 30 feet above the ground. Unfortunately, Osram's salespeople reported that maintenance managers were typically given a maximum per-bulb price by their finance directors, a price far too low to cover the cost of long-life bulbs. Finance directors would not talk to Osram salespeople, instead referring them back to the maintenance managers.

Osram's marketing people came up with a way of getting the maintenance managers and the finance directors together. They mailed a small cashbox to the finance director, with a covering letter telling them that the box contained information that would save their company £50,000 a year. The letter went on to say that the maintenance manager had the key. Keys were mailed to the maintenance managers, with a similar note. Clearly one or other manager would contact the other out of simple curiosity—opening the box provided them with the calculation on the cost savings they could make, if they agreed between them to switch to long-life low-energy bulbs.

In practice

- You need to identify the decision-makers in each organization and personalize the approach.

- Do your homework—you need to spell out to them how it will benefit their company specifically, and if possible how it will benefit them personally.

- Ensure that there is no way they can access the information without getting together.

- Make the promotion intriguing, preferably with a tangible product so that they cannot simply talk on the phone.

4 TEASE YOUR CUSTOMERS

CUTTING THROUGH ADVERTISING clutter is a perennial problem. Most people in the developed world are pretty adept at dodging marketing messages—and most marketers try to get around this simply by shouting louder, which is counterproductive, or by exaggerating their claims, which is of course even more counterproductive.

Research shows that the more someone is intrigued by the message, the more he or she remembers it and acts on it. The problem, of course, lies in generating enough interest in the message at the outset for the individual to want to hear the rest. Most marketing messages (such as press advertisements or billboards) try to get the basic message across in a few words, or even with no words, and there are many attempts to make the message stand out by using bright colors, unusual writing, etc., etc.

An alternative method is the teaser campaign, where the message itself takes a while to come through—but the preliminaries are intriguing. Usually, these are executed as billboard advertising, so that the timing of the messages can be controlled accurately, but there is no reason why they should not be executed as mail campaigns, as this example shows.

The idea

The world of textbook publishing is not the academic ivory tower one would imagine—it is a fairly cut-throat business, with publishers battling to persuade lecturers to recommend the books to the students. A good adoption can create a long-term income stream for the book, so there is a lot at stake, especially for the big markets such as introductory texts.

When my introductory marketing text was launched, the publisher's marketing manager decided to run a teaser campaign. He began by mailing out sets of chopsticks to every marketing lecturer in the country: the chopsticks were packed in metallic silver envelopes with the message "First you eat." This created an instant message intrigue—the physical product (the chopsticks) and the enigmatic message combined to create a feeling that something interesting was about to happen. About a week later, the same lecturers were sent another envelope containing a tea bag and the message "Then you drink." This further increased the sense of anticipation—what would arrive next? The next package contained a fortune cookie and a sample chapter of the book, with the message "Then you see your future."

Of course, the fact that this innovative campaign (which won an award) was aimed at marketing lecturers certainly helped—many of them used it as an example in class, and naturally then felt obliged to recommend the book—but the basic principle applies to almost any situation.

In practice

- You need a good, clean mailing list.

- Get the timing right. Too short a period, and the tension doesn't build. Too long a period, and people forget the previous message.

- Don't string it out too long, i.e., send too many messages, or people get frustrated.

- Use something tangible to accompany the message: such things often sit on people's desks for days and act as a reminder.

THE "REAL MONEY" MAILING

Mailshots are regarded by most recipients as the dark side of marketing. Direct mail is the most unpopular marketing tool—usually characterized as junk mail, it is often thrown away without being read beyond the most cursory glance to check that it isn't "real" mail, and sometimes it is thrown away unopened.

Getting people to read the mailing is the first hurdle to overcome. The advice offered to direct mail companies is often counterproductive—for example, making the envelope look enticing by using color printing, putting a "teaser" question on the envelope, and so forth—because this flags up to the recipient that there is a sales pitch inside.

The idea

One of the earliest mailshot promotions, in the 1920s, was for American insurance giant Metropolitan Life. The company sent out a mailing promoting retirement plans, and glued a genuine one-cent piece to the letter. The weight of the one-cent piece made the balance of the envelope feel strange, encouraging people to open it: the letter inside explained how one cent per day saved, at compound interest, would produce over $500 after 25 years—all from only one cent, an amount that most people would not notice.

The letter went on to ask how much better it would be if the person could save two cents a day, or five cents—or a dollar. The style was sober, as if writing to an existing customer—no sales-pitch hyperbole or advertising "puff."

The key issue in the mailshot was the one-cent piece—not an eye-catching, gimmicky piece of envelope design, but a genuine (if small) gift to the recipient of the mailing. Apart from creating an intriguing mailshot, even such a small gift as a penny makes the recipient more inclined to do business with the firm. Allowing for inflation, that penny would be worth close to 50p today, of course, so it may be worth considering sticking a larger-denomination coin to the letter. After all, with the average mailing costing around £2 a time, an extra 10p (or even 50p) for a coin that will perhaps double the response rate has to be worth trying.

Metropolitan Life became one of America's largest insurance companies, funding the construction of the Empire State Building and later being the largest investor in war bonds for funding World War II.

In practice

- Make the gift worth while. Real money will always attract more attention than yet another ballpoint pen.

- Don't be stingy. Send a coin that is worth something.

- Explain the benefits clearly, without rhetoric—you already have their attention if they are reading the mailshot at all.

- Accept that not everybody will respond—but if you get a 15 percent response you are beating the direct-mail averages by a considerable percentage.

- Ensure that you link the message to the coin—Metropolitan Life were pitching for savings accounts, but the money on the letter would work just as well for home insulation, loans, and indeed anything where the main advantage is financial.

WITHDRAW THE PRODUCT

It's a truism that we don't know what we've got until it's gone. Sometimes a product becomes so familiar that we become blasé about it—and sometimes sales fall as a result. This often happens with products that we remember from our childhood, the traditional homely products that we don't buy anymore but would hate to see disappear.

A threat to withdraw such a product could well provoke an outcry—as happened when Coca-Cola withdrew the traditional Coke recipe in favor of an "improved" recipe. Despite the fact that consumers preferred the flavor of the new formula, the company had not reckoned with the iconic status of the product (perhaps surprisingly, since Coca-Cola have always promoted the product for its traditional qualities). The lesson of Coca-Cola was not lost, however.

The idea

Salad cream is a traditional British salad dressing, having a flavor and texture somewhere between vinaigrette and mayonnaise. For almost 100 years it has been the salad dressing of choice in Britain, but during the latter part of the twentieth century it began to be replaced by mayonnaise. In 2000, H. J. Heinz announced that their salad cream would be withdrawn due to falling sales.

The media immediately leaped on the story, and the public outcry that ensued created a mass of publicity for the product. Sales revived dramatically, and the product now has its own website, complete with a chef (Dan Green) creating recipes for the product. Pouring it over limp lettuce is a thing of the past—Green offers recipes for beef wraps, spaghetti nicoise, couscous with wok-fried vegetables, and many more. The website points out that salad cream has 66 percent less fat than mayonnaise, a notable benefit in the health-conscious twenty-first century.

There is no question of the product being withdrawn now—sales have soared, and Heinz are now investing £5 million a year in promoting the brand. Ad agency Leo Burnett have produced an innovative and entertaining series of advertisements, and salad cream is now firmly back in the mainstream.

In practice

- This approach only works with well-known, iconic products.

- The news media must become involved—without publicity, there will be no public outcry.

- You must be prepared to follow up quickly with conventional advertising and other promotion when the publicity is at its peak.

- Care needs to be taken that people do not feel "conned" by the promotion.

- You may need to consider other ways to revive the product, in conjunction with the threatened withdrawal—Heinz promoted new ways of using salad cream, in innovative recipes.

FIND THE KEY ACCOUNT

SOMETIMES GOING DIRECT to your final customers can be very difficult, especially if you are looking to establish your product as the industry standard. Persuading all those different customers to accept your product becomes impossible because they would all have to agree at the same time—and each one (not unnaturally) is likely to say that they will agree provided all the others do.

Many firms end up trusting to luck and persuasive promotion, as was the case with Betamax and VHS (the competing home video systems) in the 1970s and 1980s. Eventually VHS won the battle, even though Betamax was, in many ways, technically superior. Far better is to find out who will influence (or insist on) other companies adopting the product as standard.

The idea

In 1868, George Westinghouse invented the air brake. This was an important development, because railroads were spreading throughout America and indeed the rest of the world. Railroad trains are easy to start, but difficult to stop—if the braking only happens at the locomotive end of the train, the carriages will derail, and (for a long train) the same applies if braking is applied only at the end of the train. For safety, braking needs to be applied along the length of the train, and systems of levers or cables are just not fast-acting enough.

Westinghouse's system needed to be adopted across all the rail companies, however, since each carriage or freight car might be carried across several different rail companies' tracks in its progress across America. This meant that each piece of rolling stock might be connected to any other company's stock, including the brake systems. But how to persuade several dozen companies to adopt the new system?

Westinghouse examined the routings of railroads across the country to see where the main nexus of rail transport was. This turned out to be Chicago, where rail links from the West and the prairies brought cattle to the slaughterhouses, and rail links to the Eastern cities carried the meat to the tables of New York, Philadelphia, and Boston. The same links moved manufactured goods from the East to the new towns and ranches in the West.

The Burlington Railroad was the company that had opened up the West, operating trains across the prairies: if Burlington accepted the new system, Eastern railways would have to go along as well, or would have to unload and reload boxcars in Chicago. After running a series of demonstrations, Westinghouse persuaded Burlington to adopt the system—thus forcing every other railroad operator in America to do the same. Many engineers still believe that the vacuum brake is superior to Westinghouse's air brake, because it responds faster—Westinghouse's success came from becoming the industry standard.

In practice

- Make sure you have identified the real key account.

- Be prepared to offer concessions if necessary—the key account is likely to know that they are the key to your success, and will negotiate strongly.

- All your eggs are in one basket—don't drop the basket!

- A superior product, of itself, is not sufficient: even an inferior product will succeed if it becomes the standard.

ADD SOME VALUE

WHATEVER BUSINESS YOU are in, there is a strong likelihood that you have competitors who offer something similar—and it is a racing certainty that there are alternative solutions out there for customers' problems, as seen from the customer's viewpoint. For instance, someone in the restaurant business might feel complacent because there are no other restaurants in town, but not recognize that a local cinema is competition in the "where shall we go for a night out?" category.

Adding value means finding something that will mark you out from your competitors *in the eyes of the customers you are hoping to attract*. What is good value for one person is poor value for another.

The idea

When Peter Boizot founded PizzaExpress in 1965, pizza was virtually unheard of outside Italy: there were no pizzerias at all in London. Early on, Boizot latched on to the idea of providing something extra—he started by having live jazz bands performing in the restaurants (many well-known jazz musicians got their start by playing at PizzaExpress in Soho). Nowadays, the restaurants often have live music, but many host art exhibitions or have other types of live performance. The point is the company is aiming for an "artsy" audience who will enjoy this type of added value.

PizzaExpress has a Members' Club: for a subscription (currently £45 a year) members become entitled to four vouchers a year for free menu items plus a free glass of wine, to free desserts when dining early, free entry to the PizzaExpress Jazz Club, and a £10 gift voucher for every ten meals purchased.

Offering extra value has enabled PizzaExpress to withstand competition, and to keep its brand intact in the face of the "pile 'em high and get 'em out there" approach of American pizza chains. PizzaExpress is able to charge more for its pizzas than these big chains, because the added value makes them worth while—the higher prices also deter the kind of downmarket customers PizzaExpress wants to discourage.

In practice

- Only offer added value that your target customers will appreciate.

- Price accordingly—people do not mind paying more if they are getting more.

- Ensure that what it costs to add the value is less than the premium your customers will pay.

- Promote the added value—they already know about your product.

DO SOMETHING DIFFERENT

It is an axiom in marketing that successful competition comes from doing something the competitors haven't thought of. Nowhere is this more apparent than in distribution. Often traditional distribution methods mean that customers who would like to buy are unable to do so because they cannot reach the particular outlets that the product is available from, or because they don't like the outlet for some reason.

Breaking the mold of distribution can mean getting nearer to the customers that other companies cannot reach—and it may even be possible to recruit a few customers who are currently being served adequately, but who would simply find another distribution route more convenient.

The idea

Avon Cosmetics entered a market that was traditionally served by large pharmacists, department stores, and hairdressers. For most women, this did not present a great problem—a shopping trip could easily include a cosmetics buying session in the local pharmacy, or a trip to the hairdresser's could be an opportunity to stock up on lipstick and mascara.

However, a significant number of women found it difficult to do this, either because they were housebound with small children or elderly parents, or because the stores were simply too far away. In addition, women often wanted to ask advice about cosmetics, and most pharmacies do not provide any kind of advice. Avon introduced the idea of taking the product to the customer through their door-to-door service, delivering cosmetics to women and giving advice. The Avon representatives were themselves women looking to earn some money in their spare time, often neighbors of their customers, so that a visit from the Avon representative was a social event as well as a shopping opportunity.

Avon cosmetics are sold in refugee camps in the Middle East, in housing projects in New York, in leafy suburbs in Surrey, and even from canoes paddled up the Amazon. The company's sales are several times those of L'Oréal Cosmetics, and its products appear in some surprising purses. Incidentally, Avon has proved a hit with transvestites—being able to buy cosmetics in private, and importantly to have advice about cosmetics, is a major advantage for these people.

In practice

- Don't be put off by the fact that nobody else is doing it. This is an advantage!

- Be sure who your new target market will be. Are there people who are currently poorly served by the traditional approach?

- Be careful designing your new approach. You may not have a precedent to guide you.

- Look for precedents in other industries: you may be able to learn from them.

10 RESPECT YOUR CONSUMER

MARKETERS HAVE A bad habit of talking about "the consumer" as if they are one person. Consumers are in fact all different—they are a lot like people in that respect—and they are in fact us. We all resent being patronized, but many marketers do this with astonishing regularity. People discount advertising statements (in fact in most cases they don't even read them) and most of us can spot bullshit pretty well. We are all consumers—if we can see through marketers and their cunning ploys, so can everybody else.

The difficulty is always to encapsulate the concept of customer respect in a way that staff can relate to when they are working with people. It's easy for our staff to get into the habit of seeing our customers as simply cannon fodder, or walking wallets, rather than as human beings with their own needs, wants, and skills. If you need an example, try dealing with the care workers of a friend who is a wheelchair user—or better still, use a chair yourself for a day and see how people treat you.

The idea

David Ogilvy was one of the giants of the advertising industry. He was responsible for telling us that the only sound in a Rolls-Royce at 60 mph is the sound of the clock ticking, for example. What he told his staff was equally important—among many Ogilvy-isms, two stand out. The first is: "The consumer is not a moron—she's your wife!" We have to keep reminding ourselves that our consumers are not stupid, they are people just like us.

The second one is "People do not buy from bad-mannered liars." Yet so many marketing communications (especially telephone marketing approaches) are both bad-mannered and untrue. Somebody calling from India, claiming to be called Sharon, and immediately asking about how much one has left on one's mortgage, is clearly bad-mannered and lying.

These two statements should be up in letters of fire in every marketing department in the country.

In practice

- Remember that your staff may not have the same commitment to the business that you have.

- People often forget that consumers are people too—there is nothing wrong with reminding them.

- Putting up signs to remind people has a long history—IBM's "Think!" signs, Bill Clinton's "It's the economy, stupid!" sign, and many others have worked well.

- Don't forget the lesson yourself, especially when dealing with somebody difficult!

11 PLAY A GAME

GETTING PEOPLE TO be involved with the brand means getting them to build it into their lives. One way is to encourage them to see the brand as fun, and to play around with the product—which is why car dealers allow customers to take test drives. Salespeople call this the puppy dog close: once you've cuddled the puppy, it's hard to give it back!

Obviously this is not always possible with expensive or delicate products, so if that's what you're selling you need to think of some other way of allowing people to be playful with the brand. Sometimes the internet can help.

The idea

When Panasonic launched their Lumix camera range, they needed to promote the key features of the camera—its 10× optical zoom, and its 28mm wide-angle lens. The TV advertising campaign featured the Golden Gate Bridge crumpling up to accommodate someone using an ordinary camera, and the Sphinx coming toward a photographer to show how the optical zoom makes things look better. These campaigns were wonderful and eye-catching—but any marketer knows that advertising alone is never enough.

Panasonic commissioned Inbox Digital to create an online game called Lumix World Golf. The game is based around an 18-hole game of crazy golf played around nine world heritage sites. Players can zoom in and out to judge their shots (as they would with the camera) and can win prizes, offset against signing up for the Lumix e-CRM (customer relationship management) program.

There is, of course, a "tell a friend" button so that people who enjoy playing the game can involve a friend. The game itself is quite addictive and engaging—plugs for the camera are shown between each hole, and players are congratulated or commiserated with according to how well they play each hole.

The site attracted over a million visitors, most of whom found out about the site through friends.

In practice

- The game needs to be professionally executed and slick.

- It needs to connect to the product in a straightforward but fun way.

- It should connect with other promotions to reinforce the message.

- It should ALWAYS have a tell-a-friend button.

BRING A FRIEND

FRIEND-GET-FRIEND promotions are very common, but persuading people to sell to their friends can be problematic. People often feel embarrassed to do this, and some research conducted in the 1950s by two American academics (Leon Festinger and James M. Carlsmith) brought out an interesting phenomenon: people who are offered a big reward for persuading a friend to do something are LESS likely to succeed at it than are people who are offered a small reward. This is because people offered a small reward will persuade because they are themselves persuaded—people offered a large reward do so because of the reward.

In many cases, offering a reward to someone for recommending a product makes them feel as if they are betraying a friendship—not the result the company would like, and yet many bring-a-friend schemes do exactly that, offering ever-larger rewards as a way of persuading people to pass on a friend's name.

The idea

Laphroaig is a Scottish single-malt whisky distilled on the island of Islay. It is the strongest-flavored whisky available, so for some people it is too powerful, for others it is a rare treat. Obviously the quality comes at a price—but for its devotees the price is well worth paying.

The distillery has a "Friends of Laphroaig" organization that devotees can join. Periodically, the distillery asks "Friends" for the names of three or four friends, to whom the distillery will send a small bottle of the whisky as a gift. There is nothing in this for the "Friend"—the other person gets the whisky. What it does do is enable the distillery to expand the number of people who know the product, with the added advantage that the "Friends" are likely to choose people who they think will enjoy the product. Obviously there may be some abuse of the system—choosing three teetotaller friends in order to obtain three free miniatures of the whisky is one obvious possibility—but in general people are very fair about it, because it is after all a very generous offer.

The idea can be extended in other ways—banks might offer £25 to be deposited in the friend's account, a gym might have a "bring-a-friend" day with a free gift or discount to the friend if he or she joins the gym, a hotel might offer a free room to a friend.

In practice

- The offer needs to be something that the friend will appreciate and benefit from.

- The reward to the recommender is the thanks of a friend—there is usually no need to offer anything to the recommender.

- The reward needs to connect directly to the product—a sample or a trial period, for example.

- If you do give a reward to the recommender, try to make it something they can share with the friend.

USE PROMOTIONAL GIFTS THAT REALLY PROMOTE

MANY COMPANIES USE gift promotions, and they work just as well in a business-to-business context as they do in a consumer context. However, the vast majority of sales promotions only move sales forward—they rarely have the power to make people buy more, or switch brands. The reason for this is that buyers will simply stock up in order to gain the promotion, then buy less in future weeks and months until the stocks have been used up. In the consumer context, people might switch brands temporarily in response to a sales promotion, but the vast majority switch back to their usual brand or to a new brand with an even better promotion as soon as the offer ends.

The problem for most firms lies in finding a promotion that will encourage customer loyalty and will not result in a simple switch back. Offering someone extra product for the same price simply reduces profits without creating any long-term benefits—whatever the short-term advantages might be.

The idea

Goldwell is a German manufacturer of hair care products, sold to professional hairdressers. When the company entered the British market, they were up against established professional suppliers such as L'Oréal, Wella, and Schwarzkopf: all these firms were very much larger than Goldwell, with deeper pockets, so a conventional approach was entirely ruled out.

Goldwell broke all the rules. Rather than sending salespeople to salons to get orders and following up with a delivery later, the

Goldwell reps sold direct from a Transit van. This meant that salons could obtain products instantly, a major consideration if stocks were low, and the reps were able to show people the full range of products.

Where Goldwell scored, though, was in their sales promotions. Purchases of stock resulted in being given extra boxes of shampoo or conditioner, but of products the salon currently WASN'T using. Inevitably, the salon would eventually use the conditioners, shampoos, etc., even if only because they would run out of stocks of their usual brands. Frequently, the stylists would prefer the Goldwell product, and would then order it next time—resulting in more free samples of other new products. Goldwell is now well up among the major suppliers to hairdressing salons throughout Britain.

In practice

- This approach works best in a business-to-business context, except where a loyalty card scheme or similar allows the vendor to gain a clear picture of what the individual currently does not buy.

- The free product needs to be given in a generous enough quantity for the buyer to use it regularly for a while: a couple of bottles is not enough.

- The buyer should, preferably, either be the person who will use the product, or be close to the people who will use it. The approach therefore works best with small businesses.

14 DO NOT BIND THE MOUTHS OF THE KINE

FOR MOST DIRECT-MARKETING companies, the internet has proved to be a godsend. Apart from the fact that it has increased the effects of competition dramatically as people are able to shop around extremely easily, the internet has meant that companies can reduce their workforces dramatically as people can order online and have goods delivered by carrier. Some companies even did away with their largely self-employed sales forces—the people operating from their own homes, often for small amounts of money.

Many of those firms came to regret their rashness—sometimes the on-the-ground sales force was the only factor differentiating them from millions of other online retailers, many of whom were more experienced at internet trading and could therefore compete more effectively. On the other hand, many of the salespeople became disaffected when they found the customers they had recruited were being lured into buying online, thus cutting the salespeople out of the picture and (more importantly) cutting them out of their commission. It doesn't take a marketing genius to figure out that a disaffected sales force not only doesn't produce: it can also cause a great deal of damage.

The idea

Betterware distribute household products through a network of home-based distributors, mostly working in their spare time. The basic Betterware selling system is based on a catalog: the distributors put the catalogs through letterboxes in their designated area, then call back later to take orders and (eventually) to deliver the goods. This system means that there is little or no high-pressure selling, distributors are usually selling to neighbors, and eventually a good social rapport is obtained between the distributor and the consumers.

Obviously Betterware cannot ignore the internet revolution, any more than any other firm: in fact, there are distinct advantages in taking orders online. However, the company has recognized that the main drawback of the internet is the lack of human contact, and in fact Betterware are already far better placed than most other companies to inject a human element. Therefore, Betterware not only pay commission to the salespeople for any sales made in their area, even if the orders are placed by telephone or online: they also arrange for the salespeople to deliver those orders to the customers. This establishes the salesperson in a position where he or she is able to sell more to the customer.

From the salesperson's viewpoint, this system is eminently fair. After all, the customer may well have taken the email address from the brochure the salesperson had dropped off—so the bulk of the work had already been done. From the company's viewpoint, paying the commission means the sales force are quite happy to recommend customers to buy online, rather than fighting against the company in order to take the orders themselves. From the customer's point of view, Betterware company and salespeople show a united front, which can only enhance the brand.

In practice

- Independent sales forces need to be given very precise territories in which to operate, otherwise it is impossible to allocate the commission.

- Make sure that salespeople are aware that they can actually encourage customers to shop online.

- This idea works best when salespeople are making the deliveries, because that way they make direct contact with the customers.

EMPOWERING STAFF

In most service companies, things go wrong with the customer experience from time to time. Obviously people expect this to happen sometimes—we don't live in a perfect world, after all—but companies are judged not so much on what goes wrong, but on how they go about putting things right. Usually, correcting problems is something reserved for managers or complaints handlers—which is fine, except that the customer often has to go from one person to another to get the problem fixed.

In services, the people element of the provision is obviously extremely important. In some cases, people actually ARE the service: hairdressing, teaching, entertainment, and so forth. For retailers, the staff are the company as far as the customers are concerned, so retailers need to consider hiring good "people" people in the first place. Not all of them do—and staff training is no substitute for hiring people who are polite and helpful anyway.

Combining these two elements, we see that customers who have a problem stand a good chance of being greeted by a disinterested store assistant, who refers the problem to someone else who may or may not be available and who may or may not be able to help. This will hardly enhance the customer's experience with the service—and it is extremely unlikely to result in a return visit.

The idea

IKEA, the Swedish furniture retailer, is famous for many things—stores the size of football pitches, simple Scandinavian designs, flatpack furniture, and Swedish meatballs in the store cafeteria, among others. What they have beyond any doubt, though, is committed and capable staff (whom they call co-workers). Getting a job at IKEA is by no means simple: the company is looking for people who can act on their own initiative, and who can deal pleasantly and capably with customers, so IKEA is extremely selective in who they employ.

IKEA staff are all empowered to fix customer problems immediately. Whichever employee is approached, he or she will deal with the problem straightaway, whether by replacing a faulty product, offering a reduction, or offering a meal voucher for the restaurant. Obviously staff have guidelines for what they should and should not do, but the guidelines are just that—staff are expected to do whatever is necessary to solve the customer's problem.

Because the staff are well trained, well motivated, and intelligent, they can be trusted to deal with problems. The result is actually a cost saving, because less staff time is wasted on dealing with a problem—if a free meal in the cafeteria saves even half an hour of management time, it is money well spent. The net result is that IKEA runs with fewer staff than most comparable retailers, and scores much higher on customer satisfaction surveys.

In practice

- Hire good staff to start with.

- Train them well, especially in terms of understanding the boundaries of their empowerment.

- Don't second-guess them. If they were over-generous in handling a complaint, or believed a customer who was pulling a fast one, it won't help if you start giving the staff member a hard time.

- Most people, staff or customers, respond well to fair treatment.

- Hire trustworthy people, then trust them.

16 SPEAK THE CUSTOMER'S LANGUAGE

COMMUNICATION IS NOT the straightforward process people often imagine. Although we tend to believe that communication is a linear process (someone says something, the other person hears it, the message got through) it is rarely that simple. Apart from the obvious problems of misunderstanding, mishearing, only getting part of the message, and so forth, there is the problem that people interpret messages in the light of previous experience.

Speaking the customer's language means more than just using the right words—people interpret everything by considering the source as well. Framing the communication in a way people can relate to is an essential part of designing a communication—but it isn't always easy to do.

The idea

The British Department of Transport found that around 55 teenage pedestrians a week were involved in accidents on the roads, usually caused by inattention—crossing the road while texting, filming each other on cellphones, and so forth. Research showed that teenagers consistently overestimate their capabilities as road users, and also they receive so many messages about safety and health issues they screen most of them out (especially messages from the government). The only messages that get through are those that they feel touch them personally.

With this in mind, the Department produced an advertisement that appeared to have been filmed through a cellphone camera, showing teenagers laughing in the street: the camera follows one youth as he dances out into the road and is hit by a car. The strapline says "55 teenagers a week wish they'd given the road their full attention." The ad was not created by professional movie-makers: to gain footage, the Department simply gave 14 groups of teenagers a cellphone camera and asked them to film their usual activities. The group used in the advertisement is an actual group of friends (from Stoke Newington in London) and only the final crash scene is performed by a stunt driver and stunt artist.

By using the kind of imagery teenagers use themselves, the advertisements were hard-hitting without being patronizing: the campaign got the message through. In post-tests following the ad being screened in movie theaters and on TV, 79 percent of respondents remembered the ad in a prompted recall, 95 percent said it made them rethink their attitudes to road safety, and 93 percent said it made them realize it could happen again. In the year following the ad, accidents involving teenagers fell by 10 percent.

By avoiding the patronizing "Hey, kids, road safety is cool!" type of approach, the Department produced a highly successful campaign.

In practice

- Don't try to guess what the target audience's language is—let them tell you.

- People don't like to be patronized—don't talk down to your audience.

- Remember that people think about communications, and take the source into account.

- Communication is not a linear process—you cannot assume that because you sent a message, and the other person received it, that the information has been correctly transferred.

17 BUILD YOUR CORPORATE CULTURE

MANAGERS (AND ESPECIALLY OWNERS) of businesses often lose sight of the fact that grass-roots staff are less concerned about the business than are the bosses. Their motivations and aims are often very different from those of senior management—and paying them a salary does not necessarily guarantee that they will always act exactly as management would wish.

For marketers, the problem is especially serious when dealing with the sales force. Salespeople usually work away from the company, and thus away from supervision: even though they are usually paid commission, this is no guarantee that they will actually do what they say they are going to do, go where they say they are going to go, and see the people they say they are going to see. In short, nearly everything has to be taken on trust.

The idea

Creating a corporate culture in which everyone feels committed to the aims of the firm will generate a social pressure on staff to do what they are supposed to do, when they are supposed to do it. This social pressure can be a great deal more motivating than money, or indeed anything else: the *esprit de corps* that makes soldiers go into battle is based on it.

Amway is the ultimate company for developing a corporate culture. Founded in the 1950s, Amway uses a direct sales force of over three million people worldwide (12,000 in Britain alone) to sell household cleaning products. Motivating and controlling such a diverse sales force would be impossible in any traditional way, so

Amway relies on its corporate culture—derived from American free enterprise principles—to ensure everybody is going in the same direction.

Salespeople are called ABOs—Amway Business Owners— which immediately provides a label suggesting independence. Motivational tapes and books are accompanied by regular meetings in which salespeople are given pep talks, often in an almost cult-like atmosphere. The net result is to build a feeling of being part of something big and important. This contributes to a sense of wanting to help the process along by selling more, by recruiting more salespeople, and by growing the Amway business.

Amway also supports a number of ethical and charitable activities, which further builds a corporate culture based on helping others to improve their lives. In turn, Amway salespeople can (and do) feel proud to say that they are working for Amway.

In practice

- Have a clear idea yourself of what your corporate vision is going to be.

- Communicate the vision consistently and frequently.

- Ensure that the staff can see that there is something in it for them in terms of self-esteem and the esteem of others.

- Help staff to realize the vision.

18 HAVE A STARTLING BRAND

MAKING YOUR BRAND name stand out from all the others is an obvious thing to do—yet many firms (especially small businesses) have brand names that are based on the founder's surname, or house name, or favorite pet's name. This is a classic wasted opportunity.

On the other hand, many firms try to develop memorable brand names, and often have expert help in doing so. Cutting through the clutter of short, memorable, zingy brand names is difficult to say the least.

One answer is to make the brand name controversial—but to do so without getting it banned altogether.

The idea

Controversial marketing is nothing new—Benetton's advertising campaigns show that—but getting a brand name that is controversial is more risky: an ad that oversteps the mark could be banned by the advertising authorities, which would mean losing the cost of producing the ad, but a brand name that oversteps the mark and is banned could lose the company its identity.

Enter French Connection United Kingdom. French Connection was founded in 1972 as a fashion chain, and although it did well the brand name did not exactly stand out from the many other slick names retailers were using. In 1997, though, the company hit on the idea of calling itself French Connection United Kingdom, and using the lower-case acronym "fcuk" on its goods. The effect was electric. The company produced T-shirts with slogans such as "fcuk fashion," "hot as fcuk," and (in Australia) "no fcukin worries."

The company was successful in claiming that fcuk is simply the company's name rather than a misspelled Anglo-Saxon word, but young people still bought the T-shirts.

The new brand appealed to rebellious teenagers who had not even been born when the company was founded—and when some people in authority failed to see the joke and banned the company's advertising, sales went up even further (and with reduced promotional costs as a sweetener). Being banned in Boston was a major boost to the company's American interests: in 2001, the company hung a poster saying "San Francisco's First fcuk" outside their first store in that city.

Being controversial carries risks—but in this case it certainly carried rewards as well.

In practice

- Try to be funny as well as controversial.

- Don't go too far—you might get banned altogether!

- If possible, link the controversial brand to your company's name. This will help you in defending against banning charges.

- The main appeal of controversial brand names is to younger people. This idea would not work for an older audience, or in a "serious" context such as financial services.

MAKE THE PRODUCT EASY TO DEMONSTRATE

Showing people how to use a product can be easy, or it can be hard. If the product is itself a complex one, and especially if it is one that might need specialist training to operate, the demonstration needs to be as simple as possible. Complexity of use is a major barrier to adoption—so it is worth ensuring that the product looks easy to use.

This may even need to be included as part of your product design.

The idea

When Remington first introduced the typewriter, they realized that most people would consider it to be a big investment, considering that a pen or a pencil seemed to be doing the same job perfectly adequately. The company needed to demonstrate the speed and efficiency gains that a typewriter could provide—if it could not write faster than someone with a pen, it was a pointless exercise buying the machine and learning to use it.

The company therefore laid out the top line of the machine as QWERTYUIOP so that its demonstrators could type the word TYPEWRITER extremely quickly. The rest of the keyboard was arranged to minimize the keys jamming in use, even though this slowed down the operation (the later DVORAK keyboard is much easier to use).

Remington's keyboard layout was so successful in marketing the new technology that the QWERTY keyboard survives to this day, despite being relatively inefficient: the alternative might have been that typewriters might never have been adopted.

In practice

- This works best for complex products.

- Don't be afraid to redesign the product to make the demonstrations more striking.

- The easier something looks to operate, the more likely it will be adopted.

THROW A PARTY

GETTING THE PRODUCT as close as possible to your customers is an obvious tactic. The easier it is for people to buy, the more likely they are to do so, yet a surprising number of firms put unnecessary barriers in the way—making people travel long distances, having inconvenient business hours, not offering credit, and so forth.

The ultimate convenient marketing approach is, of course, the party plan.

The idea

Selling consumer goods to people in their own homes goes back a long way. The Tupperware party has been around since 1946, and is the model for all other party plans. The original ethos behind the party plan was that it created a social obligation on the part of those attending to buy something—and at the same time allowed housewives to earn some extra cash for themselves, independently of their husbands.

Times have moved on. Party plan is now the ideal way to sell products that people would not buy in any other way—as Ann Summers has demonstrated. Ann Summers is a company that sells sexy lingerie and sex toys, largely to women: although the company has High Street retail outlets, most women would be reluctant to be seen entering or leaving, so party plan is the obvious answer. Women enjoy the "girls' night in" feel to the parties, which include party games and prizes, and feel comfortable buying sex aids.

Getting close to customers is one thing—bringing customers close to you is even better.

In practice

- Ensure that party organizers are well motivated and keep active.

- Choose products that will be easy (and striking) to demonstrate.

- Build in plenty of fun to the events—they are supposed to be parties, after all.

21 FOLLOW UP ON CUSTOMERS LATER

FOLLOWING UP ON customers after a sale is something few companies practice in any serious way, and when they do it is usually through a half-hearted "courtesy call" a few days after the purchase, in the course of which the caller makes a clumsy attempt to sell the customer something else. Car dealers rarely call their customers (say) two years after the sale with the idea of seeing if the customer is ready for a trade-in: yet this seems like an obvious thing to do, since the dealer already knows the customer's car, and will have a fair idea of its worth. This is, of course, one of the basic tenets of relationship marketing—but few companies do it.

Giving people time to recover from the experience of making a major purchase is also important—following up too quickly can seem over-eager. The typical reaction from a customer might be "I just spent £800 with you, what more do you want?"

The idea

The Futon Shop follow up on sales approximately one year later, offering add-on products such as drawers to fit under the futon, covers, cleaning, and so forth. After a year the customer has become used to the futon being around, and is ready for extras in a way that he or she was not at the time of purchase (obviously, or they would have bought the extras at the time of buying the original product). The customers have also had the chance to recover from the initial investment.

In general, customers welcome the approach, because they are ready to spend again and find the approach reassuring rather than threatening.

In practice

- You need to keep very good records, and diarize things well.

- You need something of real value to offer the customers.

- Calculating the appropriate time gap is a matter of considering the value of the initial purchase, and the type of add-on you are offering.

- Try to avoid calling it a "courtesy call"—people are wise to it, and it is bad to start off by lying to your customers.

22 LOST CUSTOMERS ARE NOT ALWAYS LOST

THERE IS A tendency to regard a lost customer as a lost cause. After all, they have walked away from your service, so they don't like you, right?

This turns out not to be the case. Lost customers probably liked some of what you did, even if they didn't like all of it: they already know you, and probably you already know them. So why not try to win them back? Obviously you will need to have a very clear understanding of why they defected in the first place, and (ideally) you should have a different win-back plan for each type of defection.

The idea

BellSouth Mobility is a major cellphone operator in southern America. The cellphone business has a high churn rate, but BellSouth Mobility recognized that its rate was exceptionally high— so it set about revitalizing lost customers. After one or two failed attempts, the company hit on a winning formula: it identified the key reasons for defection, which were (1) BellSouth did something to upset me, (2) BellSouth wouldn't issue a credit for a failed call, (3) BellSouth gave free phones to new subscribers, but not to people renewing their contracts, (4) BellSouth would not give current promotions (e.g., free calls) to existing customers.

Contracts for cellphones are renewed annually: BellSouth's first attempt was to mail 3,500 defected customers to tell them they could have a free phone and free calls if they switched back: the response was disappointing, with an average cost of $800 for every customer won back. The company revised its approach, this time contacting people who had defected 11 months previously, who would therefore be approaching the end of their contract with the new provider. Mailings were followed by a telephone call: this time around 10 percent of the lost customers returned, at a cost of $325 per returning customer. This was considerably less than the cost of recruiting new customers.

In practice

- Develop your plan around the real customer defection issues. Don't guess about these issues—research the problem by asking defected customers why they left.

- Communicate in a relevant way—you need to tell them that you know why they left, and you are prepared to make amends.

- Test your approach. Often what seems like a logical way to proceed turns out not to be—and then those customers are REALLY lost!

- Time your win-back plan to coincide with the customer's ability to return.

BAIT THE HOOK

OFTEN PURCHASES OF one product encourage purchases of another. A gift or loan of one product creates demand for something else that shows a profit. People sometimes need a little nudge to buy from you rather than from somebody else—and you can often arrange to give them that nudge at very little cost, if you just think about people's needs.

In some cases, providing a free service is enough to tip the balance!

The idea

Waitrose, the upmarket supermarket chain in Britain, are well aware that people like to throw the occasional party. They sell everything anyone would need, from invitations through to cleaning products, but of course so does every other supermarket chain. Waitrose's idea for nudging people was to offer a free glass hire service. If you're throwing a party, Waitrose will lend you the glasses, no strings attached, for free provided you bring them back clean. Breakages are charged at £1 a glass (although it's actually cheaper to buy a replacement glass from the store and put it in the box).

Obviously if someone is collecting the glasses from Waitrose the next step is to buy in the booze, the food, the napkins, the paper plates, and so forth. Few people would borrow glasses from the store and then buy everything else in Sainsbury's: the loan of the glasses shows trust of the customer, which in turn will reflect back on the store. The advantage for Waitrose doesn't stop with the sales, either—lending people things is a way of demonstrating friendship, which creates a longer-term obligation on the part of the customer.

Waitrose have even extended the scheme to cover loans of fish kettles, since most households would only occasionally need to cook a whole salmon, for example.

Waitrose have a long history of considering customer need first, then working out how to make a profit from satisfying the need. Encouraging people to have more and bigger parties is part of that ethos—and very effective it has proved as well.

In practice

- Ensure that what you are offering will not cost you too much to give. The glasses loan is actually extremely cheap, if the administrative element is disregarded.

- Don't attach any strings. If you do, the element of trust is lost.

- Accept that some people will abuse your trust.

- Ensure that the free gift or loan really does link to something that will show a profit—in the case of Waitrose, the high-margin snack foods are probably the most profitable product link.

- Be confident you can recover the loaned goods—or at least if not, that you can afford to lose them!

HOLD ON TO THOSE BROCHURES

In GENERAL WE tend to think of brochures as a way of promoting products, and so they are in most contexts. In some circumstances, though, we might be giving away expensive brochures without much hope of the prospective customer actually reading them. For example, exhibitions are places where a great many visitors simply collect brochures from every stand they can, without really having much intention of reading them (and still less intention of buying anything).

Ensuring that only genuinely interested people have a brochure is one issue—the other issue is ensuring that the company gets the maximum "bang for a buck" from the brochure. Brochures are expensive to produce and distribute—handing them out to people who will simply dump them is not good business, but nor is allowing interested parties to collect brochures from all our competitors as well as us, without ensuring that ours is the one that gets the results.

The idea

Thermastor Double Glazing was at one time the third-largest window company in Britain. They were also probably the most expensive—their patented insulation system was state-of-the-art and has not been matched before or since. Among many innovative marketing ideas, one of their best was the "no brochure" approach, used at exhibitions.

The company instructed its salespeople to tell stand visitors that all the brochures were gone, due to heavy demand from other visitors. The stand staff would then offer to mail out a brochure: only the genuinely interested would give their addresses, of course, so immediately the salespeople would have eliminated most of the time-wasters.

The next phase of the idea was that a salesperson would turn up at the address to deliver the brochure personally. Even without any high-pressure appointment-making sales script, the salesperson would have established a personal contact, and would be able to leave a telephone number or (if the circumstances seemed right) to make an appointment for a demonstration of the product.

The result of this approach was that few brochures were thrown away unread, and at least one in ten resulted in a sales call.

In practice

- This idea works best on exhibition stands or other places where a large general audience can be expected to turn up.

- Salespeople should not be too pushy when they deliver the brochure (or at any other time, in fact—people are wise to it).

- The brochures should be delivered as soon as possible after the initial contact—the next day is best, but certainly within a week, otherwise the customer might buy from a rival.

- Don't worry that most people won't leave their addresses—that is, after all, the aim of the exercise!

25 SHOW PEOPLE THE COMPETITION

MOST OF US are a little bit afraid of our competitors. All too often, they come over and eat our lunch—we lose customers to them, and if we keep on losing customers to them, we lose our business. What is easily forgotten, though, is that they are probably just as afraid of us as we are of them. After all, we have a better product, better customer relationships, and we are all-round nicer people.

So why not be up front about it with our customers? We don't have to run our competitors down, in fact that is usually counterproductive because people feel sorry for the underdog, but there is nothing wrong with telling people what our competitors have on offer—after all, it's hardly a state secret.

The idea

When Judy Kearney was director of sales and marketing at Holiday Inn, the company lost a large corporate customer to a rival hotel chain. Kearney tried persuasion, but to no avail—the lost customer was happy with the new chain. However, the decision-makers were not the people who stayed in the hotels—the guests were actually salespeople, engineers and executives on business trips. Kearney asked them if they were happy with the new hotel chain, and found that they preferred Holiday Inn.

Kearney suggested to the management that they survey their staff themselves and find out if they were happy. She pointed out that unhappy employees are unproductive employees: the company management carried out the survey and found (to their surprise) that employees preferred Holiday Inn.

This was still not enough. The decision-makers agreed to visit Holiday Inn and see the improvements for themselves, but still insisted on seeing the competition as well: this is where Kearney showed a touch of genius, plus a penchant for risk-taking.

She arranged a tour of Holiday Inn's own hotel, but also agreed to line up all the other visits on the same day, even volunteering to drive them around to the competitors' hotels. The customers were overwhelmed by this, and gave Kearney the contract—apart from Holiday Inn scoring well against its rivals, the fact that Kearney showed such faith in her own product that she was prepared to help them see the competing products was convincing, to say the least.

In practice

- Don't ever criticize your competitors—it looks like a lack of confidence in your own product.

- Let people make their own decisions, but be prepared to guide them a little.

- Go out of your way to be helpful. This builds trust, and a sense of obligation.

- Make sure you really ARE better than the competition on the factors the customer values most.

TAKE YOUR PARTNERS

Bringing in business yourself is always satisfying—but how much better would it be if other people brought business to you? Choosing the right partner organizations can make a dramatic difference to you—the right partner can do most of your selling for you, and will be more than happy to do so if it benefits their own business.

If the businesses are suitably complementary, it may be possible for you to pass business back their way—benefiting both of you even further.

The idea

Swansea Sport Flying is an ultralight flying school operating out of Swansea Airport, on the Gower Peninsula in South Wales. The Gower is an area of outstanding natural beauty, with many hotels and guest houses that are thronged with visitors each summer. Swansea Sport Flying does a roaring trade in trial lessons during the summer, when tourists take the opportunity to see the Gower from the air and also have a go at flying an ultralight (with an instructor on board, of course).

To promote trial flights, the school has an arrangement with most of the guest houses, hotels, and pubs on the Gower. The guest house has trial-flight vouchers to sell, for which they take a 10 percent deposit to firm up the booking. The customer pays the remaining fee when he or she arrives to take the flight: the guest house keeps the deposit as its commission on the deal. This keeps the bookkeeping simple, and provided the guest houses have a good supply of vouchers it is clearly in their interests to sell flights—after all, the sale of a flight is simply extra money for them, for no extra outlay. It also adds another service to their existing business, with no effort or outlay. In some cases, guest house owners have had trial lessons themselves, which of course makes them both more convincing and more enthusiastic when recommending the experience to guests.

From the viewpoint of the flying school, the trial lessons are just an extra income, for the effort of delivering blank vouchers to the guest houses, something that can easily be done on days when the weather is bad and there is no flying.

In return, the flying school keeps a list of recommended guest houses. This is available for student pilots who live far enough away from the school to make it worth while booking into a guest house—often a useful thing to do in the winter, when flying might be cancelled due to the weather and some days may only be suitable for a few hours early in the morning or late in the afternoon. Visiting pilots often also need somewhere to stay.

In practice

- Try to find a partner with a complementary business.

- Keep any cash exchanges simple—letting them keep the deposits is a simple way of sharing the wealth.

- Stay in touch with your partners, so they remember to push your business.

- Keep partners informed about any changes that might affect the way you operate together.

- If possible, let your partners try your service.

27 MAKING EXHIBITIONS WORK

MOST EXHIBITORS GO to exhibitions with the aim of making sales, meeting buyers, generating leads, and so forth, and most of them come away disappointed. The reason is simple: there are very few buyers at exhibitions. Most visitors are there for other reasons—research shows that many of them are there to sell to exhibitors, or to find out what competitors are up to, or to get new ideas (engineers and designers make up about 25 percent of exhibition visitors), or simply to have a day out (students, retired people, office administrators, and so forth all go to exhibitions).

Buyers in fact represent less than 10 percent of exhibition visitors (despite what exhibition organizers might say). Even when they are there, and are looking to buy, they will be seeing all your competitors as well.

Many exhibitors become disheartened when they find this out, and stop exhibiting. This is a big mistake: those other visitors are useful (even the students) because, after all, they do have an interest in the industry.

The idea

Because there are no buyers, there is not much point in having salespeople on the stand. Other visitors (such as engineers, administrators and so on) might be useful sources of information—so why not put your own engineers, etc. on the stand? Visitors who are not buyers might be users of your products and services, and will know who you should be talking to at their companies—often they are quite happy to provide a name for you, and even an introduction.

If you put the right people on the stand, you will make the right contacts. Almost anybody from the potential customer company can help you get a foot in the door—even retired people can probably tell you who you should be talking to, and might even give you some inside information about the best approach to take. The main thing is to ensure that you are giving the visitors something in return—if you are talking to an engineer, talk technical and give them the information they are looking for.

In practice

- Don't staff your stand with salespeople. They have the important job of following up the leads you generate.

- Remember that less than 10 percent of visitors to most exhibitions are buyers.

- Focus on your reason for exhibiting—it is to make contacts, not make sales.

- Think about the needs of the visitors. That way you have a chance of exchanging something of value.

SET THE PRICE, EVEN ON THINGS YOU ARE GIVING AWAY

IT'S AN INTERESTING facet of the human psyche that we don't value things that we get for nothing. There was the famous example of the man trying to give away £5 notes on the street—and no one accepted them, suspecting a catch.

Many organizations have free newsletters or house magazines that they send out to staff and other stakeholders, knowing that (probably) most of them end up in the bin. On the other hand, who would pay for a newsletter or a brochure from a company?

The idea

The Marketer is the Chartered Institute of Marketing's magazine. It is sent out free to all members, and although there is a mechanism for non-members to subscribe, virtually all the readers get the magazine for free. This is fairly obvious, since the circulation of the magazine is around 37,000 copies per month, and CIM has a worldwide membership of 47,000.

However, it does have a cover price on it of £10 (which is in itself enough to deter any would-be non-member subscribers). The purpose of putting a price on the cover of a free magazine is twofold: first, it gives an impression of quality that is absent from a free magazine. Second, it gives the recipients the impression that they have been given something of real value, not simply something that is cheap and disposable. For Institute members, the cost of the magazines (at £10 a time) is just over half the annual membership fee, so *The Marketer* offers a clear, tangible, and indeed monthly benefit of membership.

People are far more likely to read something that has a price tag attached, even if they did not actually pay the price—the value is clearly there.

In practice

- Don't go over the top on the cover price—it should be realistic, considering the quality and content of the magazine.

- Make sure the price looks "natural," as if it is about right for the magazine, and is no more obtrusive than it would be on a paid-for publication.

- If possible, include a subscription service telephone number. You never know—someone might actually want to subscribe, but in any case it increases the credibility of the cover price.

- This principle applies to other give-aways—free gifts with a purchase should carry a price tag.

LET THEM SHOUT!

IRATE CUSTOMERS CAN be hard to deal with. They feel let down when their product (or more often, service) goes wrong, and they want to hit back. Of course, yelling at the only person who can help them is not good policy, but it's difficult for most people not to do this, and it's even harder for the company employee or manager to take things calmly when confronted with an irate customer.

All too often, a customer complaint ends up degenerating into a shouting match between the customer and the manager—even if an employee is empowered to disconnect from the customer (for example, by hanging up the telephone or calling Security), this does not solve the problem.

Ultimately, people solve problems for themselves. If the problem cannot be resolved by talking to the person who supplied them, the customer will go to someone who can solve the problem—usually a competitor. Not only does this lose you the customer, it also generates a large amount of negative word of mouth.

The idea

The Cellular One cellphone company has 40 "save" reps in its San Francisco call center. These people have the job of saving defecting customers wherever possible: each "save" rep takes about 50 calls a day from disaffected customers, many of which are abusive.

The first step in the save process is to allow the customer to vent their anger. The reps are trained to ignore abuse, and to understand that the customer is angry about the situation they find themselves in: they are not really angry with the company, and certainly not with the "save" rep. The next stage is to work out what the actual problem is—where the service has gone wrong, in other words. For example, a customer whose calls keep being disconnected probably has a problem with the telephone rather than with the network, so reps are empowered to send out a new telephone to see if that will fix the problem.

The next step is to follow up a few days later. This is essential—if the problem still persists, the almost-defected customer will in fact defect permanently, rather than call back again. It is easy to assume that the problem is now fixed simply because the customer doesn't call back, but it is often the case that the customer has fixed the problem themselves by going to one of your competitors!

In practice

- Let the customer vent their feelings—and don't take it personally.

- Find out calmly what the root of the problem is, and offer a solution.

- Follow up afterward to check that the problem has been solved—don't assume it's all OK just because the customer didn't come back to complain again.

- Try to ensure that the same problem doesn't happen again for another customer.

TURN A DISADVANTAGE TO AN ADVANTAGE

MOST MARKETS ARE in a state of monopolistic competition. This means that one large company controls most of the market, and sets the pace, and the other companies in the market have to follow the leader. Many companies find themselves at a disadvantage when they are competing against the market leader—the leader controls the sources of supply, has the biggest advertising budget, and often controls the distribution network.

This doesn't mean the others can't compete—it just means they need to act more like judo wrestlers, and turn the leader's strengths against it.

The idea

When Avis car hire was founded by Warren Avis in 1946, the company had a total of three cars. By 1953, it was the second-largest car hire company in America behind Hertz. Somehow Avis couldn't catch up with Hertz, so in 1962 the company turned an apparent disadvantage to an advantage by adopting the slogan "We're Number Two—So We Try Harder."

This slogan is extremely powerful on a number of levels. First, it gives the immediate impression that Avis will do more for the customer than will Hertz. Second, it gives the impression that Hertz, as the market leader, is complacent and resting on its laurels. Third, it appeals to people's sympathy for the underdog. Fourth, and perhaps most importantly, it is easily memorable.

The Avis slogan is one of the best known in the world. Nowadays, the company still has not caught up with Hertz, but it is very close behind—if Avis ever did catch Hertz, of course, the slogan would no longer apply.

In practice

- Think about your main disadvantage, compared with the market leader.

- Think about how that disadvantage can be seen as an advantage.

- Express the idea in less than ten words.

- Make it punchy and memorable.

DEVELOP AN ICON

PEOPLE DON'T RELATE to products—they relate to brands. This is a good thing, provided you have a stronger brand than your competitors: but how do you get that stronger brand in the first place?

For strong brand read likable brand. If people feel warm toward the brand, they will in turn feel warm toward the product, which can only be a good thing for immediate sales and future loyalty. One effective way of building likability is to create a memorable icon, a symbol of your brand that will stick in people's minds and be entertaining.

The idea

Dry batteries have been around for over 100 years now: the first ones weighed in at over three pounds, and were used to power telephones, but technology moved on rapidly and zinc-carbon batteries became ubiquitous. At the same time, prices dropped: zinc-carbon batteries were disposable, and were in fact disposed of regularly.

When alkaline batteries appeared, they were a great deal more expensive than zinc-carbon batteries (and still are), so the manufacturers, Duracell, needed a way of demonstrating that the batteries would be cost-effective. Their initial advertising campaign showed a set of electric toy animals that gradually stopped working as their batteries ran down, except of course for the one powered by Duracell copper-top alkaline batteries. This was the Duracell Bunny, a pink toy rabbit banging a drum.

The Duracell Bunny became iconic. People responded well to the "cuddly toy" aspect because of its playfulness, and the memorable advertisements: more importantly, the key benefit of the product came across extremely clearly. More recently, Duracell have been able to do away with the other toys and use only the bunny—it has been seen climbing mountains, canoeing, playing leapfrog, playing soccer, and free running. The advertising was so successful that Ever Ready brought out their own bunny to advertise Energizer, but for legal reasons these ads have not been shown in Europe or Australia.

In practice

- Consider your unique selling proposition—what does your product have that others don't?

- Try to create a playful icon.

- Use your icon in different contexts so that it remains fresh.

32 ● EDUCATE YOUR CUSTOMERS

When a product is new, and often when it isn't, people need a certain amount of help in working out how to use it. This goes beyond including an instruction manual—sometimes there are circumstances in which the product might be used differently from the way it has been used in the past. For example, Heinz Salad Cream is now promoted as a recipe ingredient, as well as for its original use as a salad dressing.

Showing the product in use is one thing—showing it in the use context is another, and sometimes people need to be given a whole new idea for an activity involving your product.

The idea

During Britains's post-war boom of the 1950s and 1960s, Rowntree's chocolate manufacturing company were looking for a new way to shift chocolate. They came up with the idea for a chocolate-covered after-dinner mint. The only problem was that people were not (at that time) in the habit of giving dinner parties at home. Socializing usually took place outside the home, in pubs or coffee bars, rather than over a home-cooked meal.

Rowntree's therefore had to show people how to have a dinner party. The early advertisements for After Eight mints showed people enjoying a dinner together, with the hostess bringing food out from the kitchen and the guests complimenting her on the meal. The concept of an after-dinner chocolate did not exist prior to After Eights, and in fact for most people the idea of having a dinner party did not exist, either.

For Rowntree's, the combination of creating a whole new way of eating chocolate and also of encouraging a new group of people to have dinner parties meant having an entire market to themselves. No 1960s dinner party was considered to be complete unless After Eights were offered, and indeed many guests would bring them along as a gift in order to ensure that they would be on offer.

In practice

- Consider both the occasion and the product use.

- Don't be afraid to innovate—just because nobody else has done it does not mean that it's a bad idea.

- Get the concept across clearly in your advertising—show people how it's done.

- Show people—don't just tell them.

TAP INTO COUNTRY-OF-ORIGIN EFFECT

IF YOU HAVE a product that can be exported (and who doesn't?) you might be able to use country-of-origin effect to your advantage. Country-of-origin effect is the phenomenon by which products and brands are colored by consumers' opinions about the country the product comes from—and for many firms it can work greatly to their advantage.

For example, we tend to believe that Germans are good engineers, that the French produce great food, the Belgians make good chocolate, and the Americans are good at fast food. There are, no doubt, bad German engineers, incompetent French chefs, poor-quality Belgian chocolatiers, and very slow American restaurants, but the overall impression remains.

The idea

Cachaca is a Brazilian spirit made from sugar, rather like a white rum. Until recently, cachaca was virtually unknown outside Brazil, since only about 2 percent of cachaca production is exported. This all changed, however, when Sagatiba was launched onto the British drinks market in 2005.

The company's advertising agency, Saatchi & Saatchi, decided to use a Brazilian theme. The most famous icon of Brazil is, of course, the statue of Christ the Redeemer that stands on the Corcovado in Rio de Janeiro. Saatchi & Saatchi was aiming for a young audience, so it began by (controversially) hiring graffiti artists to spray images of Christ the Redeemer on walls all over the East End of London. It also commissioned an image of a pool player resting his arms on a cue balanced across his shoulders—imitating the pose of the statue.

Ultimately, Sagatiba seeks to tap into British perceptions of Brazil—hence the use of Christ the Redeemer. The British advertising bears no relationship to the way the product is marketed in Brazil (where the slogan "O que e Sagatiba?" or "What is Sagatiba?" is used in adverts showing jungle tribespeople worshiping the god Sagatiba, a Japanese monster movie with Sagatiba as the name of the monster, and even a naked man whose girlfriend says "Sagatiba" in a sultry voice). Sagatiba has also tapped into other Brazilian icons, soccer and samba drumming, but these have not played as well as the Christ the Redeemer icon.

In practice

- Ensure that the perception you tap into is the one that the target audience has of your country—this is likely to be different from your own perception.

- Test the alternatives. There may be more than one icon that you could use, but only one will be the most effective one.

- Never, ever, simply translate your existing advertising into a foreign language. Cultural differences go well beyond language.

- Always check with people who live in the country you are targeting. They may sometimes be wrong, but as a foreigner you will almost always be wrong if you try to guess how consumers will react.

34 CHARGE WHAT THE SERVICE IS WORTH

IT'S VERY EASY to think that competing on price is the most effective way to go. In fact, competing on price only cuts profit margins, especially since there is always somebody else who will be prepared to undercut you—even if they go broke in the process. It is generally much better, more profitable, and safer to compete on some other aspect, for example on service level.

In many cases, customers are prepared to pay a great deal to be given a top-class service, and nowhere is this truer than in business-to-business markets, where a service failure can be extremely costly.

The idea

Merchant ships are expensive items. They cost a great deal to build, a great deal to run, and a great deal to park in harbors. Having capital tied up is expensive—the ships are only really making money when they are at sea. Having the ship waiting around in harbor while customs officials clear the cargo documentation adds greatly to the cost of operating a shipping line—a fact that three friends (Adrian Dalsey, Larry Hillblom, and Robert Lynn) noticed.

In 1969, the three friends set up a courier service, delivering ships' documentation by air from San Francisco to Honolulu. The difference was that one of the founders traveled with the documentation, taking it by hand from the shipping company offices direct to the agents' offices in Honolulu before the ships arrived. In this way, customs officials could clear the cargoes before the ships docked. Dalsey, Hillblom, and Lynn became (of course) DHL and rapidly expanded their personal delivery service worldwide.

At first sight, the cost of sending a courier door to door with documents is prohibitively expensive, especially when compared with the postal service, which would deliver documents for less than one-hundredth of the price the fledgling DHL company charged. However, the service being supplied far outweighed the cost, especially once the courier was in the position of carrying documents for 20 or 30 clients. The cost of having documents arrive late, or documents being lost altogether, would be colossal: the 100 percent reliability of the service was worth paying for.

Nowadays we have become used to the idea of courier services. They are extremely common (especially in major cities where same-day delivery can be achieved) and often compete on price. However, DHL would not exist at all if its founders had tried to compete against the postal services on price!

In practice

- Think about what you are providing, not what competitors are charging.

- Think about what your service is worth to the customer, not what it is costing you to provide.

- Ensure that what you provide will meet customer expectations.

- Don't be afraid to look expensive (and high quality) rather than cheap (and low quality).

BE CONSISTENT

ONE OF THE main problems with services is that they are variable. Chefs have a bad day, hairstylists make mistakes, even accountants and lawyers overlook important details. The variability of services represents an increased risk for the customer—which is why people are often loyal to the same restaurant, hairdresser or accountant for many years.

Consistency means ensuring that the natural variations between the human beings who deliver the service are smoothed out or removed altogether.

The idea

For years, ever since World War II, the fast-food industry has deskilled restaurant work and standardized as far as possible. In many cases, staff levels have been reduced and systems put in that obviate the need for skilled staff such as chefs. Transferring this thinking to other service industries has been sporadic, but it is not impossible.

Etap Hotels, now a subsidiary of the giant French Accor hotels group, set out to deskill and standardize the hotel industry. Etap hotels are notable for their lack of a visible staff presence. Rooms are booked online or via automated call centers where the customer speaks to a machine, and late-arriving travelers may well find that there is no one around at all—a machine outside will accept a credit card either to book a room or as identification for a pre-booked room. The machine issues a keypad code that gives access to the room, so there is no need to issue or collect keys. The rooms themselves are basic, are easy to clean, and require minimal checking: in most Etaps there are no free soaps, just a soap dispenser in the shower. The TV remote is bolted to the bed, and there is usually no check on how many people use the room: there is one chair, one deep shelf that doubles as a desk, one electrical socket, one fluorescent light, and fixed coathangers. In other words, there is nothing to steal and not much to break. It is perfectly possible to stay at an Etap hotel without seeing another human being, except possibly other guests.

Customer satisfaction is very high—the convenience of being able to book online or just turn up more than makes up for the lack of service, and the consistency of cleanliness, room facilities, and locations (just outside major cities) makes a sharp contrast with independent hotels that are by their nature variable.

In practice

- Pass as much as possible of the booking system to the consumer using the internet or automated systems.

- Remove direct human contact—this is where the variability usually happens.

- Standardize as much as possible in terms of pricing, systems, and routines.

- Deskill the service so that variability due to skill levels is removed.

- Standardize the service offering by only having a short "menu."

LOVE YOUR CUSTOMERS, LOVE WHAT THEY LOVE

GETTING CLOSE TO the customers is a no-brainer. The better we understand them, the better we can serve them and the more likely they are to come back. However, most firms tend to think of "the customer" as being someone very different from "the staff."

Yet in many cases the people running the business have very similar interests to the people who come to spend their money there. This is especially true in retail—people working in clothes stores have an interest in fashion, people working in music stores are usually keen musicians, people who become chefs have an interest in good food, and so forth. The question is, how do we turn our love of these things into a love of the customers?

The idea

Tim Waterstone opened his first bookstore in 1982: he needed a job, having just been fired by W. H. Smith. From the start he aimed to share his own love of books. Customers were encouraged to browse, to the extent that Waterstone provided seating so that people could read the books for a while if they wanted to. There is nothing to stop someone sitting all morning reading, but in practice few people do this—they might read a few pages, or even a chapter, but (since they are obviously book lovers) most of them buy the book to read it at home. Staff are chosen for their love of books, and for their knowledge of specific types of book—they are expected to be able to talk to customers on an equal level.

Senior management appear on the corporate website almost hidden behind their favorite books: each has made a list of the books that have shaped their lives. Waterstone's staff are always helpful, always knowledgeable, not because they have been through a customer relations training course but because they enjoy sharing their love of books with like-minded people.

In practice

- Decide why you wanted to work in the industry you work in.

- Think about your customers—do they have the same interest?

- Decide what you can do to encourage their interest and help them enjoy your mutual enthusiasm.

- Now find out whether your staff and colleagues feel the same.

37 MAKE IT EASY FOR PEOPLE TO PAY

WE ALL WANT to buy things—sometimes we can't, because we simply don't have the money. People don't necessarily want to put things on credit cards, and in any case, for a high-value item a credit card might be wholly inadequate.

Hire purchase, leasing, bank loans, and the like may or may not fit the bill either—this is why part exchange was first developed, by General Motors, as a way of stimulating the secondhand car market and thus (by extension) stimulating the market for new cars.

For some businesses, finding creative ways for someone to pay for things is a marketing issue. There is an old joke about two shoe salespeople sent to the South Seas: after a week, one of them sends a message home saying, "Nobody wears shoes here. Coming home." The other one sends a cable saying, "Nobody wears shoes here. Send two containerloads immediately." A marketer would cable back saying, "Nobody wears shoes here, but they do grow wonderful mangoes. I have arranged a deal with a cannery on the next island to buy the mangoes, and with the earnings from this the islanders will be able to buy shoes. I have measured a sample of their feet, and we will need mainly size 8s, wide fitting, but we should have around 10 percent of the shipment in 9s and 10 percent in 7s. Women's shoes should be mainly flat-heeled due to the rocky terrain here."

This marketer is thinking about the customer's needs, not just the company's needs: it is fairly obvious who will do the most business.

The idea

Not one idea, but many, all from Barratt the housebuilding company. Barratt's was founded by Laurie Barratt, who is not a builder at all but an accountant. Laurie Barratt's contribution to the housebuilding scene in Britain was not so much in the building of the houses, but in creative ways of paying for them.

Barratt introduced trade-in to the housing market, buying people's existing homes so that they could buy a Barratt home in one easy transaction. Barratt introduced the idea of selling starter homes already furnished, so that first-time buyers would not have to find the money for a deposit and for furnishing the home all at once. He introduced a system of lending people the deposits to buy their homes—using a deferred loan that would not be repaid until the homeowner's income allowed. This was a major selling point during the 2008/2009 credit squeeze, when first-time buyers were unable to get mortgages unless they had a substantial deposit.

In 2008 he also introduced a price guarantee—anyone buying a Barratt home would have the price guaranteed if they sold within the next three years.

Making it easy to pay meant that Barratt went from a standing start in 1958 to being one of Britain's biggest housebuilders.

In practice

- Be creative. People can already borrow from their banks—you need to go a step further.

- Don't overstretch yourself—offering a top-up loan or deposit is fine, but ideally it shouldn't exceed your profit on the deal.

- Make it simple for people. If they can get the goods by signing a few forms, that's a lot easier than having to go to their bank to borrow money.

- Consider what people are able and willing to pay, and build your package around that.

38 CREDIT WHERE CREDIT'S DUE

NOWADAYS, WE ALL buy things on credit. Even people who claim that they never borrow money for anything will borrow to buy a house—life in the twenty-first century is all but impossible without occasionally borrowing money.

But what about people who have poor or nonexistent credit ratings? How are they supposed to manage? Obviously most of them don't do too well, but they still need to buy things, and we still have things to sell them: too many companies dismiss the poorer end of the community, but it's worth remembering that there is a lot less competition and a lot more to be gained in the market as a whole. After all, there are more poor people than rich ones!

The idea

When Littlewoods' catalog started in the 1930s, John Moores (its founder) recruited his first agents by sending a mailing to his existing football pools gamblers. At first, credit was limited, but Moores quickly saw the potential for giving credit to the agents (who were themselves creditworthy) on behalf of the end customers (who were not). The agents had a social bond with the end customers, since they were mainly friends, family, and neighbors: although they might be prepared to back out of paying a large, faceless company, they would be unlikely to cheat their friends or family.

Incidentally, Moores was already a millionaire in 1932: he set himself the challenge of making another million from the catalog business, starting with only one office and four staff. He did it by 1936.

The system of offering credit via the agent continues to this day, although in a somewhat reduced format: however, it still offers a potentially useful way forward in times when credit is tight for most people.

In practice

- Be very sure that the agents really are creditworthy.

- Recruit agents with good social networks if possible—encourage "party plan" marketing to help this along.

- Be careful not to overstretch your own credit.

- Be prepared to be ruthless in cutting off supplies to agents who get behind in their payments.

- At the same time, be prepared to advise agents who are having trouble collecting from their customers.

DON'T COMPETE

MOST OF THE jargon of business strategy is derived from warfare. Campaigns, guerrilla attacks, capturing markets, and so forth make us think in terms of killing off the opposition, seizing their territory, and establishing a new regime with ourselves as leaders. There is no reason why business should be a battleground, however. It is perfectly possible to cooperate rather than compete—provided you stay within the law.

Cooperation with non-competitors has been a common marketing ploy for many years: takeaway food outlets cooperating with video rental stores, for example, and tourist attractions cooperating with local hoteliers are obvious partners. Increasingly, though, there is a trend for competitors in the same industry to look for joint projects as a way of cutting development costs—car manufacturers cooperating on design (the Ford Galaxy, VW Sharan, and Seat Alhambra are essentially the same car). This idea can be extended considerably, however.

The idea

When Communism ended in most of Eastern Europe in 1989, Western manufacturers soon realized that there would be a relaxation of trade restrictions between East and West, and the West would be flooded with shoddy, but extremely cheap, Eastern European products. Skoda was already establishing itself in the West, and was actually producing some half-decent cars (even if the designs were somewhat old-fashioned). Their reputation for clunky reliability made them a threat, but rather than compete head-on with them, and perhaps risking entering a price war if Skoda engineers could recapture their former days of glory, VW decided to cooperate.

Investment by VW in Skoda was not just financial. VW took over Skoda in 1991 and redesigned the plant, re-educated the engineers, and cooperated with them in developing new vehicles. Unlike many West German companies, who simply bought out Eastern competitors and closed them down, VW went the cooperative route, allowing Skoda to build its own brand and ultimately to take over all aspects of car marketing, from design through to showrooms. Most other Eastern European car manufacturers have sunk without trace, while Skoda has been able to take advantage of Eastern Europe's low overheads and salaries and VW's technical assistance to flatten the opposition.

Skoda operates independently of VW, but is a means of increasing VW's customer base and shutting out possible competitors from low-cost countries. As an investment, that has to be better than competing.

In practice

- The cooperation must have benefits for both parties—make sure you're bringing something to the party.

- It should not attract the attention of monopolies regulators—you can't collude to carve up markets!

- Competitive synergies need to be apparent so that you don't simply cannibalize each other's existing markets. You should be cooperating in order to compete better against other firms.

- You don't need to buy out the competitor. You can often cooperate effectively in other ways.

KEEP THEM WAITING

THE RECEIVED WISDOM in business is that people want what they want when they want it, and if you don't supply them they will go elsewhere. This is true in 99 percent of cases—most people will move on rather than wait.

There may be a case, though, for developing a unique selling proposition based on having a long waiting list. Some restaurants do this (Rick Stein springs to mind) and some hotels (many paradores in Spain have waiting lists, especially for festival times). This works if you have something that nobody else has—a unique design, an upmarket restaurant, or (of course) the only hotel inside the Alhambra Palace in Granada.

The idea

The Morgan Motor Company is a tiny car manufacturer based in Malvern, Worcestershire. The company makes sports cars with a distinct retro feel—the flagship car, the 4/4, has been manufactured since 1936 (although it has obviously been modified and updated many times in the intervening years). It is, without a doubt, the car's looks that sell it.

Morgan maintain a waiting list of around two years for the 4/4: the car sells, new, for around £27,000 (a very reasonable price for a hand-built sports car), but one that is immediately available would fetch around £32,000. In other words, someone who agrees to buy a Morgan can sell it the day after delivery for £5,000 more than the manufacturer's price.

At first sight, this seems crazy—if the factory simply produced enough to meet demand, they could charge an extra £5,000 per car. Making people wait, though, gives the Morgan its unique selling proposition—Morgans don't depreciate.

All other cars lose value as soon as they leave the showroom, but a reasonably maintained Morgan will fetch at least its price when new, and sometimes more: Morgans from the 1930s sell for around £8,000, much more than they cost at the time. This gives the company something that no other motor manufacturer has—a product that is an investment.

In practice

- This only works if you have a clear and definite advantage over competitors already.

- The wait needs to be long enough to excite the customers, not so long that they give up.

- The product or service should be upmarket and prestigious.

- You are relying on conspicuousness—people need to be able to show off their new acquisition to their friends.

FORM A CLUB

PEOPLE LIKE TO associate themselves with the products they buy, and very often people have a great deal in common with other people who use the same products. Motorcyclists have a strong fellow feeling for other bikers, private pilots often meet up to swap stories and share experiences, and even rail commuters form associations to campaign for better service from the railroad.

Such groups are powerful—from a marketing viewpoint, they can create strong loyalties among their members (such as the Harley Owners Group, or HOG, for owners of Harley-Davidson motorbikes) or they can become a real thorn in the company's flesh, like the aforementioned rail commuters' groups.

The idea

Huggies is a Kimberly-Clark brand of disposable diapers that, as well as the basic version, offers variants such as swimming versions and Pull-Ups (used for potty training). The brand is successful in a competitive market, but one element in the marketing that gives Huggies a distinct edge is the Huggies Club.

The Huggies Club is open to expectant and new mothers, and offers discussion forums, advice from other new mothers, and the opportunity to provide feedback about Huggies products. The site avoids the patronizing "this is how to do it" approach common to many other sites—the site genuinely belongs to the mothers, and they are free to discuss anything and everything to do with having a baby and looking after it, whether it is related to Huggies or not.

Much of the site is available to new mothers without logging in, but those who want to post comments or access all of the site need to provide some basic information to register. The mothers are asked about the expected delivery date of the baby, which supermarket they usually shop in, and their names and addresses. In return, they are sent a £4 voucher to redeem against Huggies products. The information allows Huggies brand managers to tailor their marketing approach, and of course populate a database. Feedback from the site helps in tailoring new products, identifying recurring problems, and identifying new market opportunities.

Childbirth is a worrying time for most women—the excitement of having a baby is tempered by fears of not being able to cope, fears about the changing relationship between the parents, and so forth: since so many women now live far away from their mothers, aunts, and grandmothers any support and advice is welcome. Huggies have filled a gap, and at the same time developed loyalty and greater insights into their products.

In practice

- Don't be tempted to take over the site to plug the product. If you do this, you'll frighten people away.

- Use the members' personal information carefully. Don't abuse their trust.

- Give a small reward for providing the information—it's cheap at the price!

- Recruit some women to start the forums rolling. New visitors will not post to a blank site, but once it gets moving it will be self-sustaining.

- Publicize the club somewhere other than online.

GET THE LAYOUT RIGHT

IN RETAIL, THERE is a popular (and not entirely unjustified) view that the key success factor is the buying. Good buyers ensure that the right products are available in the right quantities at the right price—so that customers can find what they want at what they will regard as bargain prices.

Buying has, however, become so sophisticated that all major retailers have top-flight buyers who are all able to meet the success criteria. Major retailers such as Tesco, Sainsbury's, and Asda show relatively small differences between them in terms of what they stock and how much it costs: the only way left for these firms to compete is by cutting their already narrow profit margins even further.

The idea

Morrisons supermarket chain has come from (apparently) nowhere to challenge the majors. There are many things that Morrisons does not do as well as Tesco or Sainsbury's (for example, they have simplified their buying by keeping it central, and therefore the stores have a strong Northern element in the products on offer, without any allowance for regional products). Their prices are much the same, and if anything their range of products is less.

What Morrisons does do well, though, is have an exceptionally pleasant store layout. Morrisons calls this the "Market Street" layout: the stores are arranged like a traditional early twentieth-century street market around the edge of the store, with conventional aisles in the middle. For example, most stores have a pie shop where a bell is rung each time a fresh batch of pies comes out of the oven.

Of course, people do not buy from any store unless they think that what is on offer represents value for money, but all supermarkets offer that: what Morrisons offers is a pleasanter shopping environment unmatched by other chains.

In practice

- Look at what your competitors are doing, and do something different.

- Consider the type of business you are in—establishing a "market" type layout would not suit every store.

- Consider the image you are trying to project. Sophisticated? Traditional? Low-cost? And act accordingly!

43 AVOID ANNOYING THE CUSTOMERS

PEOPLE ARE BECOMING increasingly marketing-savvy: most people are fairly well aware of what marketers are up to, and can even use some marketing jargon themselves if necessary. People do not like to be manipulated—but they do like to buy things, and they do like a bargain.

Computer printers are a good illustration. Printers are almost given away—the prices are extremely low, and often someone buying a new computer will be given a printer for free. Printer manufacturers can do this because they charge a lot for the ink cartridges—sometimes as much as the printer cost in the first place. This has become a standard tactic, and one that customers see through, to the extent that many people now buy cloned cartridges online, for a fraction of the cost of the real thing. Of course, manufacturers try to sabotage this by changing the printers so that cloned cartridges won't work, which leads the cloners to update their designs.

Going to war with the paying customers like this cannot be a good thing. People look at the printer cartridge and cannot see value for money—so they look elsewhere. Breaking this cycle is something any sensible manufacturer would want to try!

The idea

Kodak is a company that has suffered a roller-coaster ride over the years since George Eastman first made photography simple enough for the average person to take vacation snaps. By the late twentieth century, though, electronics was taking over as digital cameras replaced film cameras. Nowadays, almost all new cameras are digital—few film cameras are still available, and even the films can be hard to find.

Kodak therefore went into the printer business, producing photo-quality printers for home photography. In 2007, the company launched its EasyShare 5300 all-in-one printer. It will print ordinary documents on ordinary paper and photographs on photographic paper, and it will work as a photocopier and as a scanner. It can even connect wirelessly to the computer so that the printer need not be in the same room as the computer.

Where Kodak really pulled off a revolution was in the pricing structure, however. The printer is relatively expensive compared with other printers, but the ink cartridges are extremely long-lasting and relatively cheap, so the running costs of the EasyShare are much less than those of other printers. To get the message across, Kodak put its own salespeople in computer stores to explain the advantages of buying a more expensive printer; eventually the company expects that word of mouth will take over as the main promotional plank.

In practice

- Remember that customers are not stupid: they understand a great many of the ploys marketers use, and see them as just that—ploys.

- If you are planning anything that lies outside normal practice in your industry, you need to be prepared to put time, effort, and money into informing customers.

- Word of mouth can be encouraged by doing something radical, but the best way of encouraging it is to have a good, effective product and an honest relationship with your customers.

WORK WITH THE NEGATIVE ASPECTS OF YOUR PRODUCT

THIS MAY SEEM perverse: after all, everyone promotes their product's positive aspects and plays down the negatives. However, people are still aware of the negatives—ignoring this elephant in the family room is likely to cause problems if you do not address it. No amount of positive promotion will overcome a serious negative, because people will assess your promotion in the light of what they already know—and if what they know about you is bad, they will simply not accept your positive messages.

The idea

When diesel fuel was first used for road vehicles, it was almost exclusively used for commercial vehicles such as buses, lorries, and some taxis. Diesel was regarded as the fuel for smelly, noisy, low-performance workhorses: the oil crisis of the 1970s changed that, with the development of high-performance diesels for cars. The greater fuel efficiency, cheaper fuel, and lower emissions meant that Continental drivers switched to diesel in their millions, but in Britain the advantages were less obvious—a small, crowded country with urban driving being the norm meant that diesel was slower to catch on.

Volkswagen saw this as a golden opportunity. VW began a campaign designed to overcome the "workhorse" image of diesel. The campaign was humorous, showing people forgetting that their high-performance VW ran on diesel—leaving notes on their own windscreens, pulling up at the wrong pump, tying knots in their handkerchiefs.

These adverts generated much higher than average recall, and VW's diesel sales rose 40 percent, making it the market leader and displacing Peugeot; 43 percent of VW's new cars sold in Britain in 2002 were diesels. The campaign was repeated in 2003 and 2004, with equally dramatic results.

In practice

- Find out what people DON'T like about your product (or about your company, for that matter).

- If you have a negative USP (unique selling proposition), try to think of a humorous way of promoting it.

- Be prepared to promote heavily.

- Don't expect instant results—it takes time to change opinions.

45 PUT YOURSELF ON A NETWORKING SITE

ONE OF THE major growth areas of the internet has been social networking sites such as Facebook and Friends Reunited. Facebook in particular has shown dramatic growth over the past few years, and has literally millions of members. These sites are visited by millions of people, but because they are essentially sites for people to meet their friends, the atmosphere is unthreatening and people's resistance is low.

The idea

There is, of course, a system for advertising on Facebook, and the advertising can be targeted to specific groups of people— your market can be segmented by age, by gender, by interests, by hobbies, by marital status, and so forth. This means that people see advertisements that are relevant to their own needs and circumstances, rather than having to accept a "scattergun" approach and therefore spending effort on filtering out advertising that is of no relevance or interest.

However, some small businesses simply say what they are doing at present (flying, sailing, serving meals, etc.) and thus communicate with friends. Provided the person running the business has enough friends on the system, word quickly spreads. Some small businesses, especially those in inherently exciting areas such as aviation, mountaineering, bungee jumping, or travel, have made great use of the social networking sites to promote their services and maintain relationships with existing customers.

In practice

- Recruit a large number of people to your list of friends. They will form the nucleus of your network.

- Upload plenty of photographs of you, your friends, your business, and so forth.

- Don't be too obvious about promoting your business—this will alienate customers, and will also provoke the site owners to start charging you for advertising.

- If you do decide to pay for advertising space, target your audience as precisely as possible. This will eliminate time-wasters.

46 DISCOURAGE THE UNDESIRABLES

MOST FIRMS SPEND most of their time trying to attract and retain customers. Most of the time, this is exactly what should be happening—but most managers (especially in service industries) are aware that some customers simply are not worth keeping. How much better would it be if they were discouraged in the first place? After all, finding out that they are not good customers involves making some effort.

The idea

Frizzell Insurance specializes in insuring people such as teachers, civil servants, and local authority workers—people who, by their career choice, show that they prefer a safe, quiet life. As motorists, these people are like gold dust, of course. Frizzell, in common with many other insurance companies, operates online and through a call center, but it is a small company and cannot handle a large influx of calls: the company therefore wanted to discourage unsuitable callers, i.e., high-risk drivers.

Frizzell's TV campaign showed couples who had insured through Frizzell for many years. The couples were shown as they are now, and as they were when they first started insuring with Frizzell, with music from that period playing. The advertising was tested with both the target audience and with the "undesirables": the target audience thought the ads were charming and engaging, whereas the undesirables thought them boring, banal, and condescending.

Frizzel experienced its biggest-ever annual growth in business, outstripping arch-rival and market leader Direct Line.

In practice

- Identify the factors that will be most likely to repel the undesirables.

- Test any advertising carefully with both the target audience and the undesirables.

- Make sure that the factors that repel undesirables do not also repel the target audience!

WATCH HOW PEOPLE ACTUALLY USE YOUR PRODUCTS

AMAZINGLY, MANY FIRMS have little or no idea of what happens to their products after they leave the factory. Yet such information is clearly vital in developing new products, and in knowing what the key benefits are of the old products. After all, if a baker found out that the main use for his rye bread was as doorstops he might consider changing the recipe.

The idea

Fisher-Price is among the world's largest toy manufacturers, especially in the toddler and younger child markets. The company, which is based in Chicago, hit on the idea of running a free crèche for pre-school children. The toys are all made by Fisher-Price: some are established in the market, others are prototypes.

What the children neither know nor care about is that they are research subjects. Trained observers watch the children to see which toys are the most popular, which are ignored, which are played with for a few minutes and then rejected, which are clung to fiercely at the end of the day, and exactly how children play with the toys.

This observational research is invaluable in developing new products and modifying old ones.

In practice

- You need to observe over a long period of time.

- If you can, video record the behavior rather than rely on memory or note taking.

- Have more than one observer—you may find that each of you interprets what you see differently.

- Observing people without their knowledge or consent is unethical, and could even land you in legal trouble—ensure people know what you are doing.

FORM A PANEL

MARKET RESEARCH IS an expensive business, and many small firms feel it is not worth it. In many cases, of course, the firm might be right: small firms are usually very close to their customers and can soon pick up what people like and what they do not like.

However, in other cases feedback from customers is not so easily obtained, and especially in cases where long-term streams of feedback might be needed.

The idea

Insight Express is a consultancy that specializes in online market research. The company has carved out a niche for itself in this type of research, but in fact the basic approach is fairly simple. Insight Express has an online panel of permanent respondents called e-RDD. These respondents are paid for their time, and are prepared to comment on any product or topic: all respondents are volunteers, of course, and the system has obvious advantages over stopping people in the street or cold-calling people at home.

Using an online panel means that responses are instantaneous, they can be analysed by computers (being already in electronic format), and the only real cost lies in rewarding respondents. The idea is fairly easy to adopt for most companies—rewarding existing customers with product is one way forward.

In practice

- Recruit a representative sample—make sure there are people in there from all the different customer types you have.

- Reward them for their time. Free product could work well. If you don't reward them, they will either not respond at all, or simply provide the fastest answers they can.

- Keep them feeling involved—feed back to them how their responses have helped you improve the product offering.

- Recruit new members as your customer profile changes.

GET SOMEBODY ELSE TO PAY FOR WHAT YOU GIVE YOUR CUSTOMERS FOR FREE

GETTING MONEY OUT of people is never easy, and it seems that the more money someone has, the less likely they are to want to part with it. Wealthy people are constantly being pestered for money—by charities, manufacturers of prestigious brands, investment consultants, get-rich-quick artists, and so forth.

Most of these people become hardened to sales pitches, and get used to dodging advertisements: getting to them is never easy, so a possible way forward is to give them something for free, no strings attached. After all, they didn't get rich by paying for things!

The idea

thisismoney.co.uk is a website run jointly by several newspapers (the *Daily Mail*, the *Mail on Sunday*, the *Evening Standard*, and *Metro*). The website carries news and views about all financial issues, whether pensions or the stock market, at no cost to the visitor. Visitors can even ask for free advice from the journalists.

The site costs relatively little to run because the stories have already been prepared for the respective newspapers—at most, they need some editing to fit the format of the website. The site is paid for by advertisers, happy to have access to a group of people who have enough money to need to go online for advice on managing it. The users of the site are, of course, wealthier than average and looking for solutions to their financial problems: most of those problems derive from having surplus cash rather than a shortage, so the group is a highly desirable one.

thisismoney.co.uk carries banners, pop-ups, and hyperlinks to other sites, all paid for by the companies concerned.

In practice

- The website must be attractive to the target audience—in other words, provide them with a very high-quality service.

- The audience themselves must be a desirable and identifiable market segment—not just any old visitors will do.

- You will still need to make some effort to sell the advertising space.

50

MAKE PEOPLE BEHAVE

PEOPLE REMEMBER MUCH better if they have to do something: putting people into a position where they feel as if they are already using the product can be a powerful way of getting them to remember the brand. This isn't always easy—car dealers do it by offering people test drives, but for many products this is simply not possible.

One way of doing it is to find a situation where people are already acting in a way that would remind them about the product, and then nudge them a little further.

The idea

Right Guard is a well-known deodorant, widely available but with many competitors. Perhaps surprisingly, there are still many people who rarely, or never, use deodorant: the problem for Right Guard was to promote daily use of deodorant in a market where the Right Guard brand is one of the market leaders.

Accordingly, Right Guard arranged to refit a whole London Underground train, replacing the straps that commuters hold with Right Guard cans. Commuters are already aware of body odors—especially when others raise their arms to hold the overhead straps. Holding the Right Guard can with arms raised in the position people adopt to use the deodorant generated a very powerful message.

Naturally, the train's interior advertising cards and exterior livery were also converted totally to Right Guard—and it certainly did no harm that "Right, Guard!" was at one time a common way of signaling the train's guard that all passengers were aboard.

In practice

- Think about how people use your product.

- Find some other activity that generates similar behavior.

- Be prepared to be creative and make an effort to create the same circumstances for people.

- Back up your promotional ploy with publicity—let the press and news media know what you're doing. Try to make it newsworthy!

51

GIVE PEOPLE SOMETHING THAT HELPS YOU TO COMMUNICATE YOUR BRAND TO THEM

SOMETIMES WE HAVE a great idea for cutting through the advertising clutter and getting right to our target audience, only to find that they lack the necessary means to receive our message. For example, running a TV advertising campaign in a country where few people own televisions is likely to end in failure—as would running a newspaper campaign in a country with low literacy levels.

Finding the perfect way to reach a target audience is not always easy: most advertising expenditure is wasted because it takes a scattergun approach, sending the messages out almost at random, with many people who would never buy the product being contacted (and often irritated) by promotional efforts.

Sometimes it is possible to give people the means to receive the messages—or even allow them to earn the means, if the medium itself is desirable.

The idea

PepsiCo's brand Mountain Dew is a popular soft drink in America and some other markets. PepsiCo wanted to target a youth market with the product, but young people are notorious under-consumers of media such as magazines and newspapers, and are also known to be marketing-savvy (especially in America, where more than half of the population have attended a marketing course of some kind).

A few years ago, PepsiCo spotted an opportunity. It became fashionable for teenagers to carry pagers (electronic messaging devices), so PepsiCo hit on the idea of running a sales promotion in which teenagers could buy a pager for a heavily discounted price if they sent ten Mountain Dew bottle tops in to the company.

The promotion was a great success in increasing sales of Mountain Dew, but more importantly it put PepsiCo in the position of having millions of members of their target audience walking around carrying a dedicated communication device. PepsiCo were able to send out promotional messages to the entire group at the touch of a button—giving them instant access to the exact people they needed to contact, at minimal cost.

The cost of the pagers was not much more than the $20 the customers paid for them: this is a self-liquidating sales promotion, because the promotion pays for itself—a great idea in itself!

In practice

- Self-liquidating promotions require you to find something that people want to buy, and that carries a high profit margin—otherwise it is not possible to offer a big enough discount to be attractive, but still cover the costs.

- Communication devices are not necessarily electronic—free magazines or newspapers would work just as well.

- Try to ensure that the communication device is valuable in itself to your target audience.

- Do not overuse the medium—you don't want people to throw the device away or leave it switched off most of the time.

52 | HELP YOUR ALLIES TO HELP YOU

In many business situations, you will have allies. These are companies that sell to the same target audience, but do not compete directly with you. For example, people who read the local paper obviously live locally and are therefore within your catchment area; having the local paper on your side would be a good thing.

Sometimes it is possible to operate on a larger scale—especially if you have a large number of possible allies.

The idea

When Tate Modern (the London art gallery) opened its doors it needed to attract the kind of audience that would enjoy modern art, and especially the kind of avant-garde exhibits that Tate Modern was planning to show.

Tate Modern's marketing team developed a profile of the type of person they thought would be in their target group (always an excellent starting point for any marketing activity). This included the type of restaurant they were likely to patronize, the type of coffee shop they would prefer, and the type of bar they would drink in—not businesses that would compete directly with an art gallery, but ones that would attract a similar audience.

Tate Modern arranged to supply Tate-branded chopsticks to Japanese restaurant chain Wagamama, and 6 million Tate-branded disposable coffee cups to the Coffee Republic coffee shop chain. Finally, the gallery supplied Tate Modern-branded beer to the fashionable Mash restaurant.

From the viewpoint of the restaurants and bars, being associated with Tate Modern was in itself prestigious: having the gallery supply them with free disposables also helped their bottom line. At the same time, getting the brand across in a novel and interesting way to 6 million coffee drinkers was achieved at a relatively low cost—this sophisticated audience would be difficult to reach in any conventional way.

In practice

- It is absolutely essential to begin by identifying your "typical" target customer—which other goods and services they buy, where they like to go on vacation, which magazines they read, and so forth. Be as detailed as possible.

- Find a giveaway that helps your allies either to sell more themselves or to save money.

- This idea works best if your allies can see an advantage in being allied to you.

- Be careful in your choice of allies—be sure that they will use your branded products effectively and in a way that enhances your status.

- Be very clear with your allies about how the partnership will work—what are the boundaries?

53 KEEP YOUR EGGS IN ONE BASKET

MARK TWAIN SAID that the wise man keeps all his eggs in one basket—then watches that basket. This can be good advice for the smaller firm: spreading the resources too thin, or trying to please everybody, is likely to end in tears since larger firms can do this effortlessly.

Specializing means cutting out competition—large firms have real trouble in specializing, not because they lack the resources but because they cannot convey a specialist brand message easily: no one will believe that they can specialize in everything.

The idea

Young's Home Brew is a specialist wholesaler dealing only in products for people who brew their own wines and beer. Young's has a website that has a section for retailers (Young's customers) and a section for consumers offering advice and information about home brewing. This provides information that may not be easily available elsewhere—for example, special yeasts are now available that will survive in alcohol strengths as high as 40 percent, creating the possibility of brewing full-strength spirits at home.

Young's has managed to establish a reputation second to none in terms of specializing in home brew. They have become the first port of call for any retailers, and the consumer site encourages more people to ask for Young's products when setting up their own home brew operation.

In practice

- Resist the temptation to try to please everybody—this will blur your brand values.

- Make sure you really ARE the expert in your chosen specialism.

- Convey your specialist status to all interested parties—intermediaries, suppliers, consumers, everyone.

- Use the internet, but not exclusively: why not contact your local TV, radio, and press to tell them you are available as an expert commentator?

- Being a specialist means you are not going head-on against the big firms. You would have to be very drunk to pick a fight with the bouncers—so why do it in business?

54 WHET THE CUSTOMER'S APPETITE

GIVING PEOPLE A free sample or a free trial is an old ploy, but in some cases it is difficult to do without giving away a great deal more than was intended: for example, offering a free trial of a credit rating service might give the potential customer everything he or she wanted to know, without the need to subscribe permanently to the service.

Finding a way of making people want the product without at the same time giving away the main advantage is a difficult tightrope act to carry out.

The idea

When Oasis (the pop band) wanted to promote their *Heathen Chemistry* album, they followed the usual route of seeking airtime on radio, of advertising in music enthusiast magazines, and so forth: obviously these routes are used by every other band, so they needed something else to attract the attention of their target audience.

The band arranged to give away encrypted CDs with four tracks from the album, attached to the *Sunday Times* newspaper. The CDs could only be played four times before they automatically wiped themselves clean, so the recipients could not replay the tracks without buying the whole album. From the sale of each album, 50p was donated to the Prince's Trust, a charity for helping young people.

This unique approach enables people to try the album without gaining possession of its key benefits, thus compelling them to make a full purchase.

In practice

- Ensure that the freebie you are offering does not contain the main benefits that the customer would want to own.

- At the same time, ensure that it contains enough benefits for people to judge the quality of what is on offer.

- As always, try to ensure that only your target customers are given the free sample, otherwise you are wasting your samples.

55 BE STARTLING IN WAYS THAT INVOLVE YOUR CUSTOMER

THE ADVERTISING BUSINESS is a cut-throat one, and agencies often need to be very creative indeed in pitching for business—after all, if they cannot promote themselves, how can they hope to promote a client?

This means that many agencies have come up with eye-popping ideas for promoting themselves, which means that other businesses might be able to recycle the ideas for their own purposes. If you are in a business-to-business marketing environment in which you need to pitch to clients, you can learn a lot from advertising agencies. There are many examples—this is just one.

The idea

Saatchi & Saatchi is a major London advertising agency, perhaps most famous for its association with the Conservative Party during the late 1970s and 1980s. However, like other agencies Saatchi cannot afford to rest on its laurels—the agency still has to pitch for business, and has done so in some remarkable ways.

When Saatchi was pitching against several other agencies for the Toyota account, it arranged to have three Toyota cars suspended from its office building. Having three cars hanging off a central London office block not only made the newspapers—it also impressed the Toyota executives when they came to Saatchi's for the pitch meeting. Needless to say, Saatchi won the account.

Hanging cars from the corporate headquarters is not, of course, possible or appropriate for every company, but it shows how some imagination and daring can achieve a startling result.

In practice

- Determine what will most interest your customer.

- Take the fight to the customer—you need to put the promotion right where they will see it, outside their business premises if necessary.

- Be daring—you cannot startle somebody without doing something very unusual.

56 IF YOU'RE ON THE WEB, YOU'RE GLOBAL

MOST COMPANIES NOWADAYS have a website of some sort, and in the majority of cases they are interactive. What many managers forget, though, is that the internet is global—which is why it's called the World Wide Web, of course.

This means that everyone from Valparaiso to Vladivostok can access your website—and many do. Even if you think you only have a local clientele, there is nothing to stop you from picking up business from anywhere in the world.

The idea

Caja Granada is a "caja de ahorros," the Spanish equivalent of a building society or a savings and loan company. It is non-profit-making, and operates almost entirely within Andalucía. Recently, however, the company has started to offer internet banking, and it does so in both Spanish and English. People from outside Spain can open accounts, but must obtain a certificate of non-residence in order to have interest paid tax-free: Caja Granada can arrange this for a small fee.

Expanding into the global market has opened up new possibilities. Deposit accounts denominated in euros can be offered to people outside Spain, which means more cash flowing into the company, which in turn means it can lend more. The company also gains a competitive edge on some banks when dealing with people who own vacation homes in Spain—which, in Andalucía, amounts to a large number of people.

Running the website in English as well as Spanish has not been without its problems—some of the translations have not worked well, and some banking terms and concepts do not transfer easily between countries. What Caja Granada has recognized, though, is that being on the internet at all means that the company is global—so they might as well take advantage of the fact.

In practice

- Check your website for terms or concepts that might be offensive to people in other cultures (this is not easy).

- Consider whether slogans will mean the same to foreigners, even when they are English speaking—most of us are familiar with differences between American English and British English, for example.

- Consider having your website translated for your main potential customers—but always use a native speaker to do the translating.

- Consider the use of your product in other countries. For example, bicycles are mainly sport items in Britain, but are basic transport in Africa.

57 LOOK BEYOND THE OBVIOUS

Most advertising managers simply book advertising space and place the advertisements. In most cases, this is perfectly fine—provided the advertisement is in the right place and says the right things. However, it is possible to make the advertising more powerful by considering the whole picture—in other words, by integrating the marketing communications.

The idea

When the Orange cellphone company finally achieved full coverage of Britain they decided to publicize the fact. The campaign, called "Covered," played around with the concept of covering things.

Orange wrapped over 40 sites, wrapping whole buildings in Orange livery. They booked anything up to 16 consecutive 48-sheet billboard sites (the largest size available) so that people would see nothing but Orange advertising for anything up to a mile. They covered whole floors in railroad stations with Orange advertising, and even recovered all the seats in the Eurostar waiting room in Paris to promote the service to Brits returning from France.

The campaign cost £800,000 in total (relatively cheap for a large company's campaign) but generated £2.73 million in return.

In practice

- Start with a good platform—a simple idea that everyone can connect with and that serves as a focus for ideas.

- Link everything back to the platform.

- Use several media and several different approaches—though without losing the central style.

FIND THE USP

The USP or unique selling proposition is what makes your product stand out from everyone else's. However, what you think the USP is may not be the same as what your customers think it is—a restaurateur might, for example, think that the quality of the food is the USP whereas it may be that the waiters and waitresses are exceptionally attractive people.

Finding the USP may involve carrying out some basic market research, but it will certainly pay off when you come to design your promotional campaign.

The idea

K Shoes is a small shoe manufacturer based in Kendal, in the English Lake District. The company is known for producing good-quality, sensible footwear rather than high-fashion shoes: K shoes last longer and wear better than other shoes, and one might be forgiven for assuming that this is about as good a USP as one could hope for.

However, some basic research among K shoe wearers revealed something else—K shoes don't squeak. Even when new. For the wearers, this was the true USP, and was (for them) a sign of the quality of the shoes.

K Shoes used this information to develop an advertising campaign in which the advantages of non-squeak shoes were promoted in a humorous way. For example, one K Shoes advert showed a wife sneaking up on her husband while he was dining with another woman and dumping a bowl of noodles on his head. No other shoes would allow her to do this.

Knowing why people buy from us enables us to play to our strengths.

In practice

- Determine your USP from the customer's viewpoint—not yours.

- Build the USP into all your promotion.

- If you don't have a USP, get one—or you won't survive long.

59 REPOSITION INTO A BETTER MARKET

SOMETIMES A BRAND has been promoted to a target audience that is disappearing, or at least turns out to be less attractive than another audience. The brand might be doing perfectly well, but could do better: this is where repositioning comes in.

Repositioning means establishing the brand in a different location in the customer's consciousness. Usually, it means changing the way everybody thinks of the brand—not just the existing customers, but anyone else who might now consider the product. The position of a brand in people's minds is always relative to other brands and products, some of which may not be direct competitors—people often say that a product is "the Rolls-Royce of . . . ," for example.

Repositioning takes time and effort, but the payoffs can be very large indeed.

The idea

Lucozade is a carbonated glucose drink available throughout Britain and in many other countries. It was originally developed as a drink for people convalescing after serious illnesses—the glucose provided quick energy, and the bubbles gave people's digestive systems a boost. As a way of nourishing someone whose appetite might be poor it succeeded very well, and was in fact an iconic brand.

However, during the 1980s it became clear that there were a great many more healthy people than sick people. General improvements in healthcare and aftercare meant that Lucozade had a shrinking market—while at the same time interest in taking up sport was on the increase as more people had leisure time to fill.

A series of TV advertisements showing decathlete Daley Thompson drinking Lucozade helped to reposition the product. Handy-sized bottles were used instead of the larger one-pint bottles Lucozade originally came in, and the drink was sold through vending machines and at sports clubs.

Nowadays, Lucozade uses Lara Croft as its role model, and the repositioning is complete. Sales have multiplied, but more importantly the product's future is secure in a growing market, rather than the shrinking market it occupied previously.

In practice

- Before deciding to reposition, be very sure that you want to lose the market you are already in.

- You cannot occupy two positions at once—if you reposition, you lose the position you already have.

- Be very clear about the position you want to occupy—consider the competitive issues particularly.

- Anticipate retaliation from competitors in the new market.

- Keep your promotion consistent with the new position.

60 USE THE PACKAGING

PACKAGING IS, AT its most basic, there to protect its contents from the environment and vice versa. However, packaging can do so much more—it can inform customers about the product, advise people about different possible ways of using the product, promote other brands in the firm's portfolio, and so forth.

Most brand managers are familiar with these aspects of packaging, and so this is all standard stuff—but some firms go further, and provide customers with some fun or extra utility from the packaging. For example, in France mustard is commonly packed in wine glasses, so that the customers can use the pots afterward. In many developing countries packaging is recycled to make oil lamps or to decorate houses. In some cases, the packaging can be designed just for fun.

The idea

French mineral water bottler Evian wanted to package its water in a plastic bottle that could be easily recycled. Most plastic bottles take up considerable space in recycling bins, even though the bottles are mostly empty space—so Evian designed a bottle that crushes down to a much reduced size.

What the company had not bargained for, though, was that people actually enjoyed the sensation of crushing the bottles. Finishing a bottle of mineral water just to enjoy crushing the bottle may seem a bit bizarre—but in fact the crushable bottle created a small, but discernible, USP in a crowded market. After all, water is water—the product relies heavily on other factors to differentiate it from its competitors.

In practice

- Watch what people do with the packaging. There may well be a good idea in there for you.

- Think of ways the packaging can add value—but remember it still has to sit on retailers' shelves.

- Packaging might be the only USP you have—exploit it!

61 INFLUENCE THE INFLUENCERS

In any market, there will be buyers and sellers. What is often missed, though, is that the buyers do not operate in a vacuum. Especially in business-to-business markets, buyers are influenced by trusted advisers: these may be work colleagues, friends, professional advisers such as lawyers or consultants, or even family members.

In some cases, influencers might be so powerful in the decision-making that the sale fails without much warning. A salesperson might imagine that everything is going fine, until the prospect's golf partner or teenage son expresses doubts about the deal or provides some piece of information that kills the deal.

Finding out who the influencers are may be easy or difficult, depending on the situation. In some cases, they will be obvious corporate advisers, in other cases they might be completely unknown to the marketer. Having the influencers onside is clearly advantageous, but how to do it?

The idea

Pharmaceutical companies have two basic markets: the over-the-counter market of drugs and medicines that can legally be sold by pharmacies and supermarkets, and the so-called "ethical" drugs that can only be sold on prescription. Ethical drugs cannot be bought by the general public, but they are, of course, stocked by pharmacists. Unfortunately, pharmacists cannot sell them without a doctor's prescription.

Pharmaceutical companies such as Merck and Pfizer therefore employ salespeople purely for the purpose of visiting doctors to promote the drugs. The doctors do not buy the drugs (apart from a few for emergency use), but they are the ultimate in influencers, because they recommend the drugs to their patients. In most cases, patients will agree to take the drugs if the doctor recommends them (although nowadays more and more people are avoiding prescription drugs), so the doctors are the targets of the major thrust of pharmaceutical companies' marketing efforts.

The principle can be applied elsewhere. Architects do not buy UPVC windows, but they do specify them; TV chefs do not sell particular cuts of meat, but they do recommend them; and so forth. In consumer markets, some major purchases may appear to be made by a wife or husband, but it is not usual for either of them to make a big decision without consulting the other one, so someone selling motorbikes would probably need to persuade the wives rather than the husbands.

In practice

- Identify the influencers in your market. In many cases, you may need to ask the actual customer if there is anyone he or she would normally consult.

- Influence the influencers by personal approaches if possible, or by promotions directed at them if necessary.

- Be subtle—influencers are usually well aware of the concept of persuasion, since this is what they are themselves engaged in.

RESEARCH YOUR CUSTOMERS

62

Knowing your customers is basic to planning to meet their needs. Yet many companies rely on gut instinct, occasional chats with customers, or unreliable and non-specific advice from trade magazines.

Running a survey is often regarded as far too difficult to undertake. Analyzing survey responses involves all kinds of mathematical and statistical expertise, for example: in fact, designing the actual questions is a much harder task, since there are too many ways in which questions can lead a respondent to the desired response. Even selecting respondents can be problematical—many people refuse to participate, for various reasons, but the researcher has to assume that those who refuse are the same in every respect as those who participate, despite the fact that we already know they differ in one important respect: they don't do surveys!

There is, however, a solution at hand.

The idea

Survey Monkey is an online survey design system. The system allows its users to set up a survey using pre-prepared question templates, choosing from more than 20 different kinds of question. Surveys are conducted entirely online, so respondents experience the minimum inconvenience and can participate at any time they find convenient.

Simple surveys can be conducted for free, but larger or more complex surveys need to be paid for (at reasonable rates). Survey Monkey will automatically analyze and collate responses, again all online, so that results come back very quickly indeed.

All a researcher needs to do is direct respondents to the Survey Monkey website and log in. This can be done by respondents at home, or on the company's premises: in the case of (say) a retail service such as a fast-food takeaway or a hairdressing salon, the company could set up a terminal and ask customers to complete the survey while they are waiting. Surveys can be made engaging and fun to do.

In practice

- Be careful when writing questions. It may be worth reading a book on research approaches before setting up your survey—after all, it's a bit late to find out it's wrong after you have run the survey!

- Always pilot any survey. Let a few people fill in the survey first, and see what problems come up—ambiguous questions, leading questions, and questions that are impossible to answer will all be flagged up by piloting.

- Get the design right and the results will follow.

- Remember that the more respondents you survey, the more reliable the results—but the higher the cost. Around 200 respondents should be fine for most purposes.

63 INVOLVE YOUR CUSTOMERS

In BUSINESS-TO-BUSINESS markets it is easy to concentrate simply on the relationship between the buyer and the salesperson. Buyers are, after all, the ones who are responsible for making the final decision on the purchase, and are the ones who will award the contract.

However, buyers do not operate in isolation. They are usually working to a specific brief, and this has been handed to them by senior managers who consider the strategic needs of the company when deciding what to buy. This decision is made in the light of what the company's staff believe is necessary for the smooth running of their own departments, as well as on factors such as strategic direction of the firm, available budgets, and so forth.

Successful companies therefore look beyond the buyer and seek to influence those who in turn influence the real decision-makers.

The idea

Cisco Systems is the world's largest manufacturer and supplier of networking equipment. The company supplies many firms in the IT sector with equipment for creating internet, intranet, and extranet systems, and operates globally.

The main users of the equipment are the engineers who set up and maintain the systems in the client companies. These engineers will encounter problems throughout the lifetime of the equipment— new uses for the systems will be needed, systems will crash occasionally, unforeseen circumstances will cause new problems or new challenges on a regular basis. Cisco Systems has therefore established a self-help online technical support system that allows engineers to troubleshoot the systems. What the site also does is allow engineers to share information and discuss problems, so that they can help each other to solve problems that they themselves may or may not have experienced.

This encourages engineers to become more involved with Cisco, and also generates word-of-mouth (more properly word-of-mouse) recommendations. It also means that, as engineers change jobs or are perhaps hired to set up systems elsewhere, they are more likely to use Cisco products in their new jobs.

In practice

- Find out who the final users of your products are.

- Find out how you can help them to make better use of your products, preferably by direct contact with your company.

- If possible, establish links between all the users of your products, whichever companies they happen to be working for.

- Remember that companies do not buy or use products—people buy and use products on behalf of companies. Address the needs of the people, not the needs of the customer companies.

64 INTEGRATE YOUR DATABASE

ALMOST ALL FIRMS keep customer details on computer. The delivery department keep names and delivery addresses, the accounts department keep records of addresses for invoices and also keep records of good and bad payers, the marketing department keep records of regular customers, salespeople keep records of personal likes and dislikes of the buyers they see, and so forth. In fact, an individual customer might feature in several databases within the same supplier's systems, with each department keeping the information it regards as relevant and useful.

Sometimes this is done in the name of confidentiality: a customer's payment record might be regarded as something that should be kept secret from the warehouse staff, for example. More often, though, it is simple territoriality—people are reluctant to let other departments in on their special information.

The idea

Carphone Warehouse is one of Britain's biggest retailers of cellphones and peripherals. Their customer-facing staff (the people in the stores and at the end of the telephone) are trained in consultative selling, in which they find out the customer's needs and then work out which of the products on offer would come closest to meeting those needs. They also needed to troubleshoot customer problems in the event of a complaint, but they lacked the necessary background knowledge to do this.

What was needed was an integrated customer relationship management system. The company installed Trillium software to integrate all the data on customers into a single database. Interestingly, this showed that some customers appeared in the company's databases more than once, perhaps under a slightly different version of their names (for example, Alan Smith might be recorded as A. Smith), so effort was being wasted on contacting the same person more than once.

The new, combined database was cleaned (old addresses removed) and de-duped (duplicate customer records removed). As a result, Carphone Warehouse staff now have an up-to-date, accurate, and comprehensive view of each customer available in real time, if necessary while the customer is in the store. This enables the staff to identify opportunities for cross-selling, and also to identify customer need more accurately.

In practice

- Find out what information exists on your customers, whether it is on computer or not.

- Combine the databases and remove any duplications or obsolete addresses.

- Ensure that confidential information is only available to those who really need it by password-protecting those parts of the database.

TAP INTO THE SOCIAL NETWORK

GETTING THROUGH TO Generation X and Generation Y consumers is a difficult task at best. They are marketing-savvy (more than half of all Americans have been on a marketing course of some sort, and Britain is not far behind), and cynical about conventional marketing. They seek control of all their interactions with companies, and have been brought up with the idea that the consumer is king—they are certainly not easily manipulated.

They have also been brought up with the internet. Anyone under the age of 30 has trouble remembering a world without cellphones and the internet, and virtually all of them are computer literate and regular net users. They have no difficulty in setting up software to block pop-ups and banners, so advertising to them in any obtrusive way is somewhere between difficult and impossible—yet at the same time they will consciously seek out information about products.

This combination of factors is causing a revolution in advertising and promotion generally. Traditionally, advertising consisted of a series of unsought communications, i.e., communications the consumer was not looking for, aimed at persuading people to buy. Now, advertising has become largely sought by the consumers, and its aim is to "nudge" the person to buy one brand rather than another when they are already 99 percent committed to buy.

But how to do the nudging?

The idea

YouTube has been one of the phenomena of the twenty-first century. It allows people to post and share videos on the internet, and literally millions of people have done so. Some of the clips are no more than a few seconds of shaky "home movies" taken on a cellphone, others are professionally produced videos. Some movie companies have put clips from their latest releases onto YouTube, and popular TV shows sometimes appear—*Shaun the Sheep* has appeared on YouTube, to name but one.

In some cases, companies have put commercials on YouTube. Strictly speaking, this is against the terms of use: YouTube specifically excludes videos that aim to solicit trade, but in general this has been interpreted to mean that the company does not allow advertising that directly seeks a response. General promotional advertising is allowed provided it is interesting and amusing for YouTube subscribers.

YouTube had 160 million unique visitors worldwide as of March 2007.

Other sites include MySpace, Google Video, and Yahoo! Video. Brands ranging from Gap to Victoria's Secret, Calvin Klein, Nike, and Adidas are all on the video-sharing sites somewhere: the medium is, of course, available to any business, no matter how large or small. Obviously, there is no control over who will (or will not) see the clip, but with so many subscribers that hardly matters. In any case, anyone who is interested will seek out the clip—that is sort of the point!

In practice

- Create as slick a video as you can. Use professionals if possible.

- Keep it humorous, or surprising, or entertaining in other ways.

- Don't patronize your audience. They are on the site to be entertained, not to be preached at.

FLOG IT ON EBAY

MARKETING IS ABOUT creating profitable exchanges. Even the word derives from the kind of street market that represents the ultimate in buyer–seller interaction. Street markets are dying out in most industrialized countries due to the economies of scale that exist for large firms (whether retailers or manufacturers).

Taking a product direct to market has many advantages, though. It means that the supplier and the buyer can get together without any intermediaries, which means that it is easier to get a clear idea of what customers want and need. It means that middleman profit margins are taken out of the equation (although wholesalers and retailers usually earn their profit margins by increasing efficiency). It means that the seller has more control over the whole process, in conjunction with the buyer.

Doing the whole thing online has obvious advantages.

The idea

eBay has been around since 1995, and was originally founded as an auction site for consumer-to-consumer deals. At the time, it was more like an online jumble sale or auction than a true street market—but since then things have moved on.

Many companies now sell goods on eBay. The site allows companies to set up "booths" from which they can sell goods, at a fixed price rather than through an auction. Having a booth can be extremely cost-effective, especially considering the number of potential customers you might reach.

In practice

- eBay customers are likely to be price-sensitive bargain hunters. You may need to keep your prices down.

- eBay has strict rules—you need to be sure you understand them and agree with them.

- This idea works best for well-known brands. Remember that potential customers cannot easily inspect the products.

- Be prepared for people to return products they are not happy with, as they would in any other mail-order situation.

COMMUNICATE IN A RELEVANT WAY

SOMETIMES THE PRODUCT'S unique selling proposition can be tedious. Whatever the real benefits, it is sometimes just not exciting enough for consumers to get worked up about. Injecting some excitement is often a matter of being creative about the advertising message—and turning a drawback into an advantage.

The idea

Grolsch is a Dutch beer aimed at mature males who consume premium brands. The beer itself tastes pretty much like any other Dutch lager beer, and during the 1990s it became marginalized by the more aggressively marketed Stella Artois, Budweiser, and Kronenbourg 1664 brands. The company's advertising agency, The Leith Agency, was tasked with repositioning the brand in order to double sales by 2002, and replace Kronenbourg 1664 as the number two premium brand by 2010.

The distinctive feature of Grolsch is that it is brewed more slowly than other beers. This gives it a fuller flavor, but telling consumers that it is brewed longer for a fuller flavor is a message that came across as dull and not very relevant. The agency identified the consumers' prevailing view of the Netherlands: that it is a laid-back, easygoing place. This perception of the Netherlands and the Dutch is what the agency hung the campaign on.

The new campaign featured a Dutch hero showing that things are better when they are not rushed. The first advert showed bank robbers attacking a bank that was only partly built. The Dutch hero shouts "Schtop!" and the endline "We only let you drink it when it's ready" was flashed up on the screen.

The end result was that Grolsch exceeded the planned sales target of doubling sales by a margin of 75,000 barrels (a 58.4 percent increase overall). By combining country-of-origin effects with the product's USP, The Leith Agency created an award-winning, and business-winning, campaign.

In practice

- Take a look at your advertising slogans and check if they are boring. If you've been using the same one for more than three or four years, it's probably boring.

- Find a humorous or startling way to convey the USP.

- Look for a further feature of your product to link the USP to—for example, place of origin, the way it is made, the age of the firm, and so forth.

DEVELOP YOUR BRAND PERSONALITY BY LINKING IT TO A REAL PERSONALITY

BRANDS HAVE PERSONALITIES of their own. It is quite possible for people to say what kind of person their favorite brand is, and in many cases people feel closer to brands than they do to real people.

Linking the brand to a specific human being has a long history. Kentucky Fried Chicken (or KFC as it is now known) is linked to its founder, Colonel Sanders. McDonald's have Ronald McDonald, and of course many British brands have the Royal Warrant. However, it is quite feasible, and even desirable, to make an even closer link with a personality.

The idea

Terry's Chocolate Orange has been around for over 70 years now. It is a ball made up of segments of chocolate-coated orange-flavored filling. The chocolate orange has traditionally been a Christmas item, with most of the promotion taking place during Advent, and millions of children being given a chocolate orange on Christmas Day. Terry's realized that the product had potential for year-round sales if it could be promoted better, so the company's advertising agency (BMP) began by identifying the brand's personality. They found that the chocolate orange is associated with the happy times at Christmas, with an indulgent playfulness. The celebrity the agency chose to represent the brand was comedienne Dawn French, who is known as a chocoholic with a sense of fun. The strapline "It's not Terry's—it's mine!" was always delivered as she grabbed the chocolate orange for herself.

The campaign was highly successful in repositioning the chocolate orange as a year-round treat.

In practice

- Begin by determining the consumer's perception of your brand personality.

- You don't need a celebrity (although it helps if you can afford one). A person who can convey the same personality as the brand will still be effective.

- Expect to invest in the promotion of your new brand personality.

- Beware of people who might prove controversial—if your real person turns out to be a criminal or a drug user it may affect your brand adversely.

69. KNOW YOUR CUSTOMER'S MOTIVATIONS

IF WE KNOW what makes our customers tick, we can offer them solutions that will appeal to their innermost motivations. Sometimes we need to look beyond the obvious—for example, few men buy aftershave, and few women buy sexy underwear. In the case of aftershave, most of it is bought by women to give as a gift to their husbands or boyfriends, and sexy underwear is bought by men to give to wives and girlfriends. This is part of the fantasy of what we would like our partners to be—less smelly, and more sexy.

Likewise, most men (left to their own devices) probably would not buy deodorant. Deodorant is not a gift purchase, though, so manufacturers need to consider why a man WOULD buy deodorant. What is the motivation?

The idea

Lynx deodorant is the world's biggest-selling deodorant spray for men. In most of the world it is sold as Axe, but in Britain that brand name was already registered so it had to have a new name. The brand owners, Unilever, decided that the only reason men buy deodorant is because they think it will make them more attractive (or at least less repellent) to women.

The company therefore developed the concept of the "Lynx effect." In the advertisements, a geeky-looking guy sprays himself liberally with Lynx and is immediately mobbed by women. The ads are tongue-in-cheek, of course: no one really expects that women are that easily persuaded, but subconsciously the message gets through that smelling better will improve your chances with women.

The idea actually grew from an earlier Unilever product, Impulse. This was a body spray for women, and the advertising showed men doing something romantic after catching a whiff of the Impulse-sprayed woman—for example, chasing after her down the street with a bunch of flowers. The motivation is similar: while the Lynx-sprayed men enjoy the idea of a lot of sexy women chasing them, the Impulse-sprayed woman enjoys romantic encounters with attractive, non-threatening men.

In each case, the key lies in finding out what the real motivation is for buying the product.

In practice

- Find the hidden motivator. Is it sex? Security? Respect of others? Often these are totally separate from the apparent "surface" motivation.

- It is OK to make the advertising a bit of a fantasy. Nobody really believes advertising anyway—it all operates on the subconscious level.

- Make the characters in your advertising believable. People relate best to people who they perceive as being like them.

<table>
<tr><td>**70**</td><td></td></tr>
</table>

IDENTIFY YOUR COMPETITORS—AND LEARN FROM THEM

IT'S VERY EASY to lose sight of the real competition when you're battling it out for market share. For many years, the airline industry was dominated by the big national carriers, who maintained a near monopoly on air travel by the simple expedient of controlling landing rights at major airports. Governments colluded in this in order to protect their own carriers: foreign aircraft would only be allowed landing rights in exchange for landing rights in their own countries, so that (for example) British Airways would only be allowed to fly from London to Milan if Alitalia was given rights to fly from Rome to Manchester.

When deregulation of the air began in the 1970s and early 1980s, these companies had to compete against one another. However, focusing on national carriers meant that they almost (but not quite) failed to notice the advent of low-cost airlines.

The idea

One of the key benefits of low-cost airlines (apart from price) is that bookings can be made online. This allows people to book their flights at any time of the day or night, from any location where they might have internet access. Apart from the lower air fares, this is a key competitive advantage.

Major carriers could compete by allowing online access, but nine of the European majors decided to go one step further and set up a joint online booking service. Opodo thus became a virtual travel agent, allowing people to book flights from anywhere to anywhere on whichever airline ran the route.

Opodo is not limited to bookings on its owners' flights only. This would limit the usefulness of the site for the consumers, so Opodo can book on virtually any scheduled airline in the world apart from the low-cost airlines. Opodo searches over 400 airlines to find the cheapest flights, but will also allow frequent flyers to specify the airlines they wish to use if they want to add to their loyalty points. Opodo is able to do something the low-cost airlines cannot match—it can book the entire route, even when this means switching airlines.

In practice

- Identify the key competitive advantage—it isn't necessarily price.

- If necessary, be prepared to cooperate with other firms in the same industry.

- Don't limit yourself to selling only your own services, if you can offer a better package for consumers by selling for other people as well. You'll still make money!

- Be prepared to learn from competitors, but you don't have to copy everything they do.

71 PICK THE SEGMENTS NOBODY ELSE WANTS

THERE IS A tendency for firms to aim for the most attractive groups of customers all the time—the wealthiest, or the youngest (on the assumption that they will have a longer life as customers), or those with the highest usage rates for the product. This is fine, except that everybody else is targeting the same groups, so you can expect some fierce competition.

This was particularly the case for the older consumers. Companies assumed that elderly people on pensions would have little money to spend and would probably already have most of what they wanted. What these companies had not noticed is that many older people have generous occupational pensions, low fixed outgoings (having paid off their mortgages, and having relatively few loans) and also more leisure time to enjoy activities.

The idea

This is the market Saga tapped into. Originally, Saga targeted the over-60s, offering vacations that catered for people who were prepared to pay a small premium for extra care. Saga understood their customers' needs—while they ensured that less mobile people got the help they required (for example, older Saga customers rarely need to carry their own baggage), they also recognized that most people in their sixties are fit, active, and interested in adventures. Saga moved vacations for the elderly away from coach trips to Blackpool or the Lake District toward adventure breaks in the Amazon Rain Forest and activity weekends. The company also retains a greater degree of flexibility than other package companies—recognizing that many Saga customers have children or siblings living abroad. The company allows people to combine a tour of (say) Australia with the possibility of staying on for a few weeks afterward in order to visit relatives.

Focusing on a segment nobody else wants means having the opportunity to capture the entire segment with little or no competition—Saga are now able to offer many services other than vacations to this age group, having established their credibility in the market.

In practice

- Know your segment. Get to understand their needs in detail.

- Find a segment nobody else wants—even people with very little money still buy something.

- Look for opportunities to sell a wider range of products to your segment—in other words, base your approach on the segment, not on the products you want to sell.

PICK A CARD

Encouraging people to shop in the same stores regularly has a long history, going back to the trading stamps of the 1950s and 1960s. Trading stamps could be collected from retailers and saved in special booklets, which could in turn be swapped for goods. In Britain, the Green Shield Stamps scheme was at one time the biggest outlet for bathroom scales in the country, since bathroom scales required the lowest number of books of stamps. (Incidentally, Green Shield eventually grew into Argos, the biggest consumer durables retailer in Britain.)

In the digital age, loyalty cards have become ubiquitous. Almost everybody who deals with the public offers some kind of scheme to encourage them to return and buy again—some schemes work extremely well, others simply seem to act as a giveaway. Making the scheme work well for the company can be a challenge, especially since most people carry several loyalty cards and cannot really be said to be loyal at all.

Loyalty schemes, all too often, become a glorified sales promotion in which regular purchases build up to a discount off the next purchase. A well-run scheme, though, presents a great many more possibilities.

The idea

One of the earliest loyalty schemes in Britain was the Tesco Clubcard scheme. Holders of Clubcards hand the card to the cashier on each trip, and are credited with points that can be redeemed periodically against purchases.

Where Clubcard goes a step further than most is that Tesco keep an exact record of each holder's purchases. This enables the company to build up a virtual picture of what the individual buys, how often he or she buys, and how much each person spends on an average shop. Tesco use this information to tailor their offers to the individual: each customer is given a separate set of offers, easy to do with desktop publishing software.

At first, Tesco would identify products that the individual rarely or never bought, and promote those: however, it quickly became clear that people were not redeeming those offers (presumably because these were products they actually did not want to buy), so Tesco shifted the emphasis toward special offers on products the individual does buy, or on close substitutes. Response rates rose dramatically, again demonstrating that meeting customer needs is the route to success in any business.

In practice

- Keep good records of your loyalty scheme customers. The information will help you to sell more to them.

- Promote products that they actually want to buy, rather than products you need to shift.

- Tailor your offers to the individual.

TRUST YOUR CUSTOMERS TO HANDLE THEIR OWN COMPLAINTS

VIRTUALLY ALL FIRMS have some kind of complaint handling procedure, frequently one that has many rules and constraints attached to it. The procedures are often time-consuming and therefore costly, apart from the difficulty of deciding how much compensation a given complaint should attract, or even whether the complaint is justified at all.

Most of us are familiar with the scenario in which we don't offer the complainant enough and a dispute ensues—sometimes the result is a lawsuit, but always the result is a lost customer. It is, in fact, the customers who decide whether the complaint has been adequately addressed—so why not let the customers decide what the compensation should be?

The idea

Granite Rock is a company that supplies building materials (mainly aggregate, concrete, cement, sand, and the like) to construction companies. The products are fairly homogeneous between firms—cement is cement is cement, in other words. Granite Rock therefore had a problem in establishing a unique selling proposition that would distinguish it from its competitors.

What the company does is unique. It allows customers to handle their own complaints. On all its invoices is a statement to the effect that the invoice is what Granite Rock thinks it has earned, but customers are welcome to pay what they think the company has actually earned—in other words, if a customer thinks a delivery was late, or a product was defective, he or she can deduct an amount from the invoice to compensate.

As in most business-to-business markets, buyers rely on having good relationships with their suppliers, so few (if any) abuse the system. In fact, Granite Rock has found that the overall cost of dealing with complaints has dropped dramatically: apart from the savings in terms of administration time, customers are actually awarding themselves less compensation than Granite Rock would have been prepared to pay.

The bonus is, of course, that customers trust Granite Rock and are much happier to do business with it than they are with (often cheaper) competitors.

In practice

- This works best in business-to-business markets, but should also work well in consumer services.

- Abuse is of course possible: if a customer is consistently abusing the system, it is open to you to stop supplying that customer. After all, they were probably abusing your old system anyway.

- Monitor what the scheme is costing and compare back to your previous system, but remember to include any increase in business resulting from the increased trust customers have in you.

FIND THE LOST TRIBE

Although we like to think we have moved on a lot from the days of living in the jungle, human beings still retain most of their instincts from our cave-age past. For example, we like to be part of a tribe. Anthropologists recognize that urban people still develop tribal groupings, complete with rituals (secret handshakes, special language or jargon, even special clothing), in order to have a sense of fitting in.

In our hunter-gatherer days, being part of a tribe was essential to survival: fighting off predators and finding food would have required a good-sized group. In modern times, being part of a tribe (whether it's a local street gang or a Rotarian group) is essential to our social well-being, and certainly helps us to survive better.

Tapping into tribal associations offers marketers a chance to create fierce loyalty as well as selling to a larger group than might otherwise be the case, at no greater expense or effort.

The idea

Tatoo is a French telecommunications company, specializing in pagers and cellphones. Pagers were, at one time, the communications tool of choice for teenagers throughout France. Tatoo decided to target the product at primary social groups (groups of friends and family) and so they used images of in-line roller skaters to promote the product. "Tribes" of in-line skaters were recruited to appear in the adverts (rather than use professional actors) so that the adverts conveyed an authentic image to the teenagers.

Tatoo rapidly became the biggest pager supplier in France, and followed on to become one of the largest cellphone companies.

In practice

- Identify the primary groups—these are groups of friends and family.

- This idea works best if your product helps the group to function better together.

- Consider all the other products the tribe uses so that you can identify the tribe members, and sell them other things.

FIND THE RIGHT PARTNERS

For small firms, breaking into overseas markets can seem to be almost impossible. Overseas customers naturally favor face-to-face meetings with people who speak their language, and are likely to be biased in favor of local suppliers anyway, if they exist at all.

Although the internet has helped somewhat, this still puts the onus on the customer to hunt around for a supplier—which they may not be prepared to do to any great extent if there is a perfectly good local supplier already on hand.

Finding a partner to distribute your products in a foreign country is obviously the way forward, but how is it done?

The idea

Tyron is a British company that produces a run-flat system for vehicle tires. In the event of a tire bursting (or being shot out) the car can continue to run on a steel ring inserted in the wheel. This would enable, for example, a VIP to escape from a kidnapping attempt or terrorist attack.

Tyron clearly has a large potential market in the world's trouble spots, but lacked any way of accessing the markets, at least within their minuscule marketing budget. The company therefore contacted Trade Partners UK, a government-sponsored organization that helps companies find partners overseas.

Trade Partners UK arranged for Tyron's salespeople to be sent on training courses in dealing with overseas customers, and arranged for the managing director to attend key trade fairs. Tyron appointed lead distributors in ten countries and won £110,000 of immediate orders.

In practice

- When appointing distributors always agree a minimum amount that they will sell of your product. You don't necessarily have to hold them to it afterward, but it does give you the option to cancel the agreement if they do not perform.

- Use government agencies. The government want to help exports— and it is a way of getting something back for your taxes!

- Having appointed distributors, be prepared to support them with sales brochures, advice, technical support, and so forth.

TAILOR YOUR PRODUCTS

It is an axiom of marketing that we need to identify the needs of specific groups of people. Segmenting the market correctly is the first stage in planning any marketing activities, in order to offer a product that will meet the needs of the segment and will thus have a market.

In some cases, though, it is possible to take things further and actually tailor the product to the exact needs of an individual. The drawback is, of course, cost: a tailor-made suit costs a great deal more than an off-the-peg suit, simply because it requires a much greater amount of work from the tailor. In some cases, though, tailoring the product can be relatively simple—which will provide a powerful USP for the company.

The idea

In the 1980s the PC revolution was taking off, with many people buying computers for home use. A computer is a fairly complex piece of equipment, but is in fact built from a series of modules: it is not all that difficult to plug in different modules to the basic system in order to create a tailor-made product.

A 19-year-old student figured out how to sell tailored computers directly to customers, using modular assembly in a subcontracted factory. Customers could specify exactly what they needed, with advice from the company if necessary, and the machines could be assembled and dispatched within days.

The 19-year-old student was Michael Dell. Nowadays, Dell computers are sold online as well as by telephone and mail order, and they constitute one of the three largest suppliers of home computers. Dell is able to supply laptops and PCs, custom-built to the client's exact specifications.

In practice

- Technical support and advice is crucial to this idea. People know what they need, but often do not know what they want.

- Quick turnaround is important: customers might well be prepared to accept a less well-tailored product rather than wait weeks for perfection.

- People will pay more for a tailored product, but not a lot more: make sure the extra cost of tailoring is more than covered by the premium people will pay, or by the extra business that results.

77 INTEGRATE COMMUNICATIONS

In RECENT YEARS, the hot topic in marketing has been integrated marketing communications. Marketers try to ensure that every message coming from the company is (at least broadly) telling the same story. This is extremely difficult to achieve in practice—salespeople say whatever they need to say to make the sale, different media give different slants on the message, and of course the company's employees talk to friends and relatives about the company and its products sometimes with devastating effect.

One way of coordinating the messages is to use them to direct people to the corporate website: here the real messages can be set up.

The idea

Nine West Shoes needed a cheap and simple way to direct potential customers to the company's website. Getting people to visit a website about shoes is not easy at the best of times—shoes are not always the most exciting products, and people are unlikely to go out of their way to find a site about them.

What Nine West did was to mold the web address into the soles of the shoes. Thus, when someone wearing Nine West shoes left a footprint (after stepping in a puddle, for example), the print promoted the shoes.

Using one medium, especially an innovative one, to direct people to another one is not new—"As Seen on TV" used to be a popular message on point-of-sale materials in retail stores. What Nine West have done is create an innovative way of promoting their website.

In practice

- You must integrate the message at all levels in the company, from managing director to tea lady.

- All communications should have common visual standards.

- Your marketing communications strategy needs to be clear to everybody.

- Always start with a zero budget—add to it as you see what needs to be done.

- Marketing communications have to be built around buyer behavior and customer contact points.

- Build relationships with customers, and build brand values.

- Ensure you have a good marketing information system so that you can monitor the process fully.

- Ensure that you always use the same artwork.

- Be prepared to change if it isn't working.

SHARE THE WEALTH

EVERYBODY WANTS TO grow the business. Gaining more market share, winning more customers, and (ultimately) making bigger profits are all goals the directors eagerly aim for.

For most firms, though, restraints on capital limit the rate at which the company is able to grow. Working capital quickly runs out, and in any case most small firms rely on borrowed money that has to be paid back on the nail—unlike major firms, which can sell shares and only have to pay out if the company is profitable.

There is, however, a way to break the deadlock—franchise the business format.

The idea

In the early 1950s, Holiday Inns started in America. The company had a good business format, and developed a clear brand image that conveyed a mid-range, comfortable hotel for business users (during the week) and family users (at weekends).

The problem for the company is that new hotels are expensive items. Building a hotel is costly and time-consuming, but Holiday Inns did not want to go the route of buying up existing buildings since they wanted to retain their branding intact.

The answer was to franchise the format. Holiday Inns are almost all owned by the people who run them. The parent company helps prospective franchisees to find appropriate sites, build the right hotel, train the staff, create the appropriate decor, and market the hotel. For the franchisee, being given a complete business format dramatically reduces the business risk (and goes down well with the bank, too), and also allows the hotel to tap into Holiday Inns' existing branding and reputation.

From the viewpoint of the parent company, franchising has allowed a much more rapid growth than would otherwise have been possible. Franchisees pay fees and royalties for being allowed to use the format, and although the overall profit per hotel might be lower than would be the case for directly owned hotels, Holiday Inns are able to open an average of one hotel per day somewhere in the world. There is no question that Holiday Inns could never have grown as rapidly as they have without franchising—being prepared to share the idea, and the wealth.

In practice

- Your business model must be proven to work.

- You will need to allow early franchisers in at a lower rate than you would like to charge later ones—after all, you are still an unknown quantity.

- You must have a very clear manual, covering every possible circumstance: apart from the need for franchisees to know how to operate, this will ensure you keep your brand values intact.

- Accept that you will have to provide a lot of support in the early stages, but regard this as an investment in the future.

THINK SMALL

MOST RETAILERS LIKE the idea of being big. Big stores run more efficiently, operate with fewer staff, and can carry a wider range of merchandise. Stock can be bought in larger quantities, which of course makes purchasing more efficient, and it's easier to make an impact on the customers.

However, as with many other aspects of marketing, it often pays to swim against the tide and do something that other people aren't expecting.

The idea

There are many locations in the country where small premises are available. Rail and bus stations often have kiosk-sized locations, and many High Streets have small store units. In some cities, there are arcades containing small units, and many shopping malls have hole-in-the-wall space for rent. Often these can be picked up cheaply— but what retailer would be interested?

During the 1980s several companies began to locate specialist retail outlets in these tiny store spaces. One of the most successful was Tie Rack. Tie Rack opened in 1981, specializing in ties (of course), which are small, high-value items. Although Tie Rack outlets were tiny, they could still carry a much wider range of ties than mainstream retailers such as department stores: Tie Rack were able to compete very effectively in high-footfall areas such as rail stations.

Doing something the others aren't doing is basic to marketing strategy.

In practice

- Think outside the box.

- Look for a potential resource that is currently being underused or ignored altogether.

- Specialize—only very large firms can try to be all things to all people.

- Don't compete head-on with the big boys.

BE THE EXPERT

WE WERE ALL brought up with the axiom that the customer is always right. The customer is not always right, of course, but he or she is always the customer, and they decide whether they like what we are offering or not.

In most cases, the customer's preferences should be accepted and provided for—but there are some circumstances in which the provider must be the expert. This is the case for doctors, dentists, and piano teachers—they are the acknowledged experts, and it is their expertise we are paying for.

If we could establish ourselves as the experts in any given field, we should be able to command higher prices, greater respect, and more loyalty from our customers.

The idea

Up until the 1960s, ladies' hairdressers were simply technicians who did exactly as their customers told them, usually without question. The profession was low-paid and low-status, with salons competing largely on price and with little incentive to raise the standards through training.

In the early 1960s a young Jewish hairdresser from London's East End decided to change all that. He developed a system of precision cutting that meant that the hair naturally fell into shape without the need for complicated setting or perming techniques. The technical breakthrough was only the first part of the story, though—the young man followed it up by insisting that customers had their hair cut the way he thought it should be cut, not the way they wanted it cut. The young man's name was Vidal Sassoon, and his approach transformed hairdressers from technicians to artists almost overnight.

Sassoon was, of course, phenomenally successful: he now has salons throughout the world and has several training schools where he trains stylists from other salons in his techniques. Strangely, this doesn't hurt his business at all: the stylists go back to their customers proud to have trained at Sassoon's, which in itself enhances the brand image of Sassoon.

In practice

- Establish yourself as the expert by being the expert—know your business inside out and backward!

- Be firm but polite—don't allow anybody to leave your business premises with anything you are not personally happy with.

- Always explain why you are doing what you are doing.

- Always get the customer on board. Don't become confrontational.

81 ADS ON CARS

CUTTING THROUGH ADVERTISING clutter is a perennial problem for marketers. Most people avoid adverts unless they are looking for something specific: people switch channels during TV adverts, flip the pages of magazines to get past the ads, and talk through advertising breaks on the radio.

There are many ideas for getting past this process, some of which work well and others that simply irritate the paying customers—but some of the best ones involve putting the message exactly where the interested customers will see it.

The idea

Most people find driving an expensive necessity. There is little one can do while driving except look at the other cars—which is not usually all that interesting either. This does raise an opportunity, though.

Recently, several firms have appeared that can arrange to have private cars liveried (decorated with advertising messages). The motorists are paid a small amount for having their cars liveried, and naturally this helps defray the costs of motoring. Of course, the drivers are allowed to choose the companies—it would hardly be appropriate for a vegetarian to advertise McDonald's—but in general there are few problems of this nature.

The key advantage for the advertiser is that the cars will be seen in traffic, in parking spaces, at golf clubs, and so forth: sometimes this is a way of reaching people who would otherwise be difficult or impossible to contact any other way.

The ads are applied as a plastic wrap, so they can be changed easily: drivers are chosen on the basis of the cleanliness of their cars and the kind of places they go, so it is perfectly feasible to advertise on golfers' cars or on frequent flyers' cars if the company wants to approach that type of audience.

In practice

- Adverts need to be punchy—often observers will only have seconds to see the ad as a car drives past.

- Choosing the type of driver is often crucial, because this will determine the audience for your advertising.

- If possible, recruit drivers who are already fans of your product— this gives them an excuse to talk about you to their friends and acquaintances.

82 GO TO THE SOURCE OF CUSTOMERS

CUSTOMERS DO NOT just magically appear. Often they develop their specific needs over a period of time—perhaps as a result of a training program, or as a result of growing older, or simply because needs develop.

In some cases it is possible to recognize a point at which someone will become a potential customer, and help the process along. In other cases it is simply a matter of identifying a cusp and being there at the right time.

The idea

The Ikarus C42 is an ultralight aircraft with a difference—it looks and flies exactly like a light aircraft. It has a cabin heater, is more spacious than a Cessna, and can be flown on an ultralight pilot's license (which requires less stringent medical examinations and less regulation generally).

The problem is the price. The Ikarus sells for over £50,000 fully equipped, so it is not an aircraft the cash-strapped ultralight community will flock to buy. The British distributors, Aerosport, hit on the idea of selling the aircraft at a discount to flying schools so that pupils would learn on the C42. They appointed the schools as regional dealerships, so that as pupils got their licenses it would be easy for them to carry on flying the C42, either by buying one outright or by forming syndicates with other graduating pilots to buy shares in one.

Some schools set up their own share schemes, in one case offering one-twentieth shares in the aircraft, bringing the cost down below

£3,000 for the would-be pilots—well within the budgets of even the poorest ultralighter.

In practice

- Identify the point at which the need will appear.

- Do whatever you need to do to be at that point when it happens—in this case, supply the training aircraft.

- Make it easy for your customers to buy from you.

83

MAKE YOUR CUSTOMERS LAUGH

MAKING PEOPLE LAUGH has always been a good way of getting them to like you. The same is equally true of companies—humor is often used in advertising, especially for "fun" items such as toys or beer.

For some products, humor is less often used but can still be very powerful. Jokes aimed at an educated, better-off audience can often be subtle—and in particular can generate some positive word of mouth as the jokes are passed on.

The idea

BMW manufactures upmarket cars for wealthier drivers. Normally, car advertising is serious—it usually emphasizes the emotional aspects of ownership (the style, the comfort, the feeling of power) but sometimes discusses technical, practical aspects of ownership such as fuel economy, emissions, maintenance scheduling, and so forth.

Each year, on April 1st, BMW runs a spoof advertisement, usually talking about some major new technical breakthrough in the design of the cars. For example, one year the company advertised that new European Union regulations banning right-hand-drive cars from Continental Europe had caused BMW to invent a car with no steering wheel, directed by the driver's head movements. The ad warned against turning around to talk to back-seat passengers, and flagged up the dangers of looking at passers-by or interesting views. Another year the company announced the invention of a windshield coating that caused flies to bounce off, and in yet another year they announced a car that would automatically give the owner's microwave oven a call so that dinner would be ready on arrival home.

These adverts certainly created an impact at a relatively low cost, but more importantly they generated word of mouth and great memorability. People showed the adverts to their friends—something that would be very unlikely to happen with any other approach.

In practice

- If your product is upmarket, don't be afraid to be subtle.

- Press advertising is relatively cheap and offers a semi-permanent medium so that people can show their friends the joke—at the same time, joke adverts for the press are easy to produce.

- Be sure to make it clear at the end of the advert that it is a joke— also, try to ensure that someone who actually believes it would not be hurt by the misunderstanding.

FOCUS ON THE KEY ISSUE FOR YOUR CUSTOMER

84

PEOPLE JUDGE WHAT we do by their own criteria—not by ours. Knowing what the critical factors are is a key element in marketing success—and it isn't always easy to spot.

Retailers often focus on the virtual price war—the battle to persuade customers that they are cheaper than anyone else. However, this is not always the most relevant issue from the customer's viewpoint—there are many other factors involved in choosing which retailer to favor with our business.

The idea

Tesco supermarkets have many good ideas for gaining a competitive edge. Price is only one of the elements in their approach—like all the other major grocery retailers, they have to keep their prices keen, but this does not in itself provide a competitive advantage.

One of the elements that customers find important in supermarkets is the length of time spent queuing. Queuing up to pay for goods is frustrating because the customer wants to take actual possession of the shopping—not to mention move on to the next of the day's tasks.

Tesco guarantee that they will open more checkouts if there is more than one person ahead of you in the queue, until such time as all the checkouts are open. The system is monitored at Tesco headquarters: every 15 minutes, every till in the country freezes until the checkout operator enters the number of people in his or her queue. If there are more than two people in the queues for more than 5 percent of the time, the store manager is asked for an explanation. Managers are expected to be able to estimate the demand at the tills by monitoring the number of people in-store at any time.

This type of thinking is what has propelled Tesco to being the number-one British supermarket chain. Caring about what CUSTOMERS find important is the key.

In practice

- Find out what your customers think is important—if necessary, ask them.

- Pay attention to customer grumbling. There may be a solution to the problem that neither you nor they are aware of.

- Don't assume. Ask.

- Sometimes the solution is easily attained—but if not, you should calculate the cost–benefit trade-off and if necessary look for a cheaper solution.

- Pleasing your customers can only be a good thing.

VARY THE AMBIENCE

Most people in service industries know the importance of getting the ambience right. Having the right lighting, the right decor, the right smells, and even the right customers are all part of an old story. Some ambiences encourage people to linger, thus exposing themselves to more opportunities to buy, while others encourage customers to eat and run—fast-food restaurants are typical of this type of ambience.

But what happens if you have a business where there are many peaks and troughs in demand during the day? How can the ambience be changed?

The idea

Hard Rock Cafe is a music-themed restaurant chain. The restaurants serve American-style fast food, to the accompaniment of rock music, with the diners surrounded by rock memorabilia such as Jimi Hendrix's guitar or the rough notes for a Beatles song.

The restaurants are open pretty much all day, but of course there are peaks and troughs in demand—at lunch and dinner times the restaurants are hardly able to fit everyone in, and there are queues down the street: in the afternoons, things quiet down a lot and the restaurants empty. Hard Rock therefore use the music to change the ambience: during busy periods, they play fast rock 'n' roll, making diners eat faster and even getting the staff to move more quickly. Once the rush is over, the music slows down, and ballads or slow songs are played. Those diners who do not have to go back to work settle down for another coffee or a dessert, and a more relaxed atmosphere prevails. As the evening trade picks up, so does the pace of the music.

There may be many other possible ways of changing the ambience, but music is a quick and easy way—and of course it fits neatly with the restaurant theme.

In practice

- Consider the peaks and troughs in your business. How predictable are they? How much warning do you get?

- What factors in your ambience can be changed easily? Heating? Smells? Lighting?

- How would you expect the change in ambience to affect your customers and staff?

GRAB THEM EARLY

GETTING TO POTENTIAL customers ahead of the competition is a key factor in success—the first company into a market can often win a lot of business before the others are out of bed. Being first in also carries risks, of course.

One market that is definitely worth getting into early is the mother and baby market. Babies pass through various stages of development extremely quickly in comparison with adults—no sooner are they teething than they are finished with diapers and starting on their first books.

There is therefore a premium on approaching mothers as soon as the baby is born—sooner if possible.

The idea

The Bounty Bag is a pack of free gifts supplied to new mothers in maternity wards. The Bounty Bag is almost the first thing mothers see after seeing the baby—and it is a very powerful device indeed.

The Bounty Bag contains samples of all kinds of products for babies, everything from baby formula through to diapers and gripe water. Almost invariably mothers will try the products and read the brochures as well—after all, there isn't much to do while lying in a hospital, and in most cases new mothers are very aware of their lack of experience, and will be prepared to read anything that might help in finding out how to look after a baby.

The Bounty Bag is regarded as a nice perk for mothers, but it has a great deal of success in getting products to the mothers before they see the competition.

In practice

- Determine the point at which customers will be sensitized to your communications.

- If possible, join with other companies to approach the customer at that point—it makes the approach more powerful.

- If you can, follow up on the initial approach—if there is any way of obtaining potential customers' names and addresses, grab it.

BE CHILD-FRIENDLY

87

CHILDREN ARE, OF course, a key market in their own right. However, their parents are equally important, and yet many service companies do not provide very well for parents with small children. Amazingly, some retail clothing chains put the children's clothing upstairs—so that mothers with pushchairs or towing toddlers find it almost impossible to visit the children's department.

Being child-friendly might mean more than just providing a family room or putting fish fingers on the children's menu. Some businesses go a great deal further—with excellent results.

The idea

Blue Kangaroo is a London restaurant that is truly child-friendly. The restaurant management decided early on to center everything around the children—which, as any parent knows, is pretty much where the parents have to be anyway.

Downstairs in the restaurant is a play area that is monitored on closed-circuit TV. Parents can eat upstairs, away from the noise but still able to check on their children. Alternatively, there is an eating area next to the play area where parents and children can eat together, before the children go back to playing and the parents enjoy a dessert or coffee.

The children's menu recognizes that many urban children have sophisticated eating preferences: all the adult food can be provided in child-sized portions, but even the dedicated children's menu has fish goujons (rather than fish fingers) and salmon fishcakes.

The food is organic, which may reflect the parents' preferences rather than the children's, but which still shows an awareness of parental concerns.

Prices are reasonable for central London, and the restaurant opens well into the evening.

In practice

- Don't regard children as an add-on: they are far more than that to their parents, and you should respect that.

- Children are more sophisticated nowadays than ever before, and can recognize when they are being patronized.

- Children do need to burn off energy: if you don't give them the opportunity to do so, they will do it anyway, perhaps in ways you would prefer they didn't.

- The family market is so poorly catered for in Britain that there are many opportunities out there.

88. UNDERSTAND HOW YOU ARE JUDGED

In SERVICE INDUSTRIES it is easy to imagine that we are being judged on our core product. Hairdressers think they are being judged on the hairstyle, restaurants think they are being judged on the food, and so on. Often the customers have a different viewpoint, however, and as with everything else in marketing we need to consider our customers' viewpoint ahead of our own.

Finding out how people judge us is not always straightforward, but sometimes we can get a very good idea from reading the kind of advice people are being given.

The idea

Restaurant critic The *Artful* Diner suggests that people examine the restrooms of the restaurant. If the restrooms are dirty, it is extremely unlikely that the kitchens will be clean—after all, the restrooms are the part of the restaurant you are allowed to see, so how much worse will be the parts they are not allowing you to see?

A survey carried out by London Eats found that 29.4 percent of Londoners thought that the cuisine was the most important factor in choosing a restaurant; 20.8 percent thought that recommendation was the most important, 18.3 percent thought price, 10.7 percent thought ambience, 10.7 percent thought service was most important, and only 10.2 percent thought location was most important.

In practice

* Read newspapers and magazines that carry reports about your industry, for an idea of what your customers are being advised.

- Ask customers what they like about you. If you can, ask your competitors' customers what they like about your competitors.

- Work out ways of improving people's perception of you.

- Whatever they regard as important is what you have to get right—other factors are less important, no matter how much you might regard them as essential.

89 ## INTRODUCE A THIRD ALTERNATIVE

PEOPLE HAVE MANY ways of judging value for money, but most of us will tend to judge by comparing with other similar products. Since price is also used as a surrogate for judging quality, people often simply go for the middle price—they tend to assume that the cheapest product is probably not very good quality, and also that the most expensive one is too luxurious or not good value for money. This creates a problem for companies with two products in their range—which one will customers go for?

The idea

Continental AG is a German-based vehicle tire manufacturer. It has a very substantial share of the market for tires fitted as original equipment to BMW, Mercedes, and Volkswagen cars, as well as supplying tractor manufacturers, truck makers, and bicycle manufacturers.

For the general public, Continental supplies tires under its own name and under the Uniroyal brand for the premium end of the market, under the Semperit brand in the mid-range, and under the brand names of the companies that fit tires. The result of this is that customers will have at least three prices to choose from: few choose the highest price, and equally few choose the cheapest, so the Semperit brand has a very large share of the replacement tire market.

In practice

- Decide which of your competitors poses the most competition.

- If they are cheaper than you, introduce a more expensive version to run alongside yours—this makes theirs look like the downmarket version.

- If their product is more expensive than yours, introduce a "value" version so that theirs looks like the overpriced version.

- As always, beware of retaliation!

90 PLACE YOUR PRODUCT

WHEN PEOPLE SEE TV adverts they usually switch channels, go to make a cup of tea, turn the sound off and read a book for a while, or indeed anything except watch the ad. This makes it difficult to get the message across—the message literally falls on deaf ears.

On the other hand, people do watch the actual programs and movies. They also notice products being used as props in those movies—which is where product placement comes in.

The idea

Movie producers and TV producers are always looking to cover their costs. If they can get products donated to use as props, they will gladly accept them: more importantly, of course, they usually charge money for featuring products.

For smaller companies, it is unlikely to be possible to pay for a product to be integrated into the script (as BMW did for the Bond movies), but it may be possible to give a free sample to a TV or movie company to feature.

Coca-Cola is a company that uses product placement in a big way: almost all American movies feature Coca-Cola somewhere, if only as a billboard in the background, and Coca-Cola even bought Columbia Pictures in 1982: Coca-Cola Entertainment has its finger in a lot of TV and movie interests.

There is no need to be Coca-Cola to place products, though. In Britain, companies can legally give products to TV producers provided no money is exchanged, and since any and all products might be useful in a TV show or movie there are openings for everyone.

In practice

- Find out which company actually produces the shows you're interested in (check the credits at the end of the show).

- Try to establish a relationship with the producers.

- This idea works best if your product is fairly eye-catching.

- TV shows are easier to get into than movies, but some low-budget movie companies might be interested.

- Be patient. Remember that TV shows are often made a couple of years before they are broadcast.

91 SPECIALIZE TO CHARGE A PREMIUM

MANY COMPANIES THINK that being the cheapest is the way forward, yet very few people consistently buy the cheapest options. If we did, the most popular cars in Britain would be either cheap Eastern European imports or Citroën 2CVs. In fact, the most popular tend to be mid-range vehicles such as Ford Focus or Toyota Yaris.

Equally, there is plenty of room at the top of the market—there are plenty of wealthy people, or even just people who would like a bit of a treat—to fill the stores with "luxury" goods. For marketers, there is no such thing as a luxury item—everything represents value for money, and meets a specific need.

Even so, wealthy people didn't get rich by throwing money away, and they appreciate a bargain as much as the next person. This is where specializing comes in. A company or brand that specializes in catering for the wealthy needs to cut out the downmarket customers altogether, otherwise it will have an image problem.

The exception to this rule has, traditionally, been airlines. The typical transatlantic 747 has the economy passengers at the back, the business-class passengers at the front, and the first-class passengers upstairs. Apart from a higher class of in-flight meal and a more comfortable seat, though, it can be difficult to see why someone would pay the extra to fly first class.

The idea

L'Avion is a business-class-only airline flying between Paris or Amsterdam airport and New York. The airline only has business-class accommodation, but in other respects it operates very much like a low-cost carrier: passengers book online, they can check in online, and tickets are issued electronically. Flights cost upwards of €1,000, but this is cheap compared with other multi-class airlines, and of course operating costs are lower because there is no need for the airline to carry different meals, plan around different cabin configurations, and so forth.

Perhaps more importantly, no one gets an upgrade. Passengers on L'Avion will never find themselves sitting next to somebody who has paid less than a third of the business-class fare and been lucky enough to be upgraded.

In practice

- Be sure that you are really providing an upmarket service—whatever your prices, you still need to give good value for the money.

- Make sure you have a strong brand, and don't be tempted to dilute it by offering lower-price alternatives.

- Remember that price is often used as a surrogate measure for quality—people believe that if they pay more, they will get more.

92

DEVELOP A SEPARATE BRAND FOR EACH MARKET

BRANDS ARE THE personality of the product. They appeal to a particular segment, and what suits one segment will not suit another. Very few brands are able to cross between segments—people get to like specific brands, and (of course) dislike others.

Sometimes firms will use an overall brand to "wrap" the others— Heinz is a good example—and sometimes firms will use a single brand to cover a wide range of products (as Virgin does, very successfully), but in most cases firms use a separate brand identity for each product-segment match.

Sometimes, though, the product has to function in very much the same way as all the other products if it is to work with those other products.

The idea

Nokia is one of the largest manufacturers of cellphones in the world. As such, it has a range of cellphones at various prices to suit various pockets: within each country, and even between most countries, the function of the cellphones has to be compatible with the cellular phone infrastructure, so there can be little variation in performance.

However, as with nearly every other product, there is a segment of wealthy people who are prepared to pay more simply to have a product that is exclusive, i.e., excludes the rest of the population.

Nokia wanted to tap into this market, but the Nokia brand does not carry the right image for this upper-crust group.

Nokia therefore introduced a new brand, Vertu, to cover its upmarket cellphones. These are, as one might expect, seriously upmarket: although the "works" have to be the same as in any other Nokia cellphone, the exteriors are diamond-encrusted works of art. Vertu phones are priced between £4,000 and £15,000, so they are certainly not for the average adolescent text-messager.

In practice

- Consider whether your product or service could appeal to another segment if value could be added.

- Always develop a separate brand for each segment—this will take investment, but it will be worth it.

- Don't assume that people will only buy more of something if it's cheaper.

93

USE OPINION LEADERS

LAUNCHING NEW PRODUCTS is always a problem—people don't have much to base a judgment on when deciding about adopting a new product, and often new products just sink without trace. Marketing theory says that opinions are formed either from direct experience or from seeing what the leaders do—but figuring out who the opinion leaders are, and getting to them, can be difficult. For example, drinks manufacturers often give free samples to bar staff in nightclubs because the customers assume that the bar staff will know what's good to drink: encouraging the bar staff to drink a particular brand is likely to lead to positive word of mouth to the customers.

In some cases, though, firms can go a lot further, by using high-profile opinion leaders.

The idea

When Häagen-Dazs ice cream was first launched in Britain, the idea of an upmarket ice cream had not yet been explored by the general public. The ice cream was promoted as a luxury, sensuous brand but it still needed something else to spark people's imaginations.

Häagen-Dazs gave away free samples of the product at society events such as Henley Regatta, Wimbledon, polo tournaments at Cowdray Park, and so forth, with the result that millions of TV viewers saw the aristocracy eating Häagen-Dazs ice cream. Although people do not necessarily copy aristocrats blindly, the impression of an upmarket, luxurious brand was conveyed extremely effectively, enabling the company to establish itself in a new niche in the market.

In practice

- Identify the opinion formers by observing how people behave toward them.

- Consider how the opinion formers relate to the brand you are trying to launch.

- Look for opinion formers who are in the public eye—in other words, opinion formers who can be seen using the product. Don't rely on word of mouth.

- Ensure that the opinion formers have an ample supply of the product!

94

LINK TO A CAUSE

BUSINESS—AND ESPECIALLY marketing—often gets a bad press. Marketing is often associated with manipulation, persuasion, and separating people from their cash—whereas, of course, marketers see themselves as providing products and services that people want to buy.

Although marketers talk about putting the customers' needs at the center of everything they do, this does not mean that they are Mother Teresa: customer centrality is simply the best way of getting people to part with their money, in a world where they have unprecedented choice. The trick is to get people to spend with us rather than with someone else, while at the same time looking like decent, caring people.

The idea

Cause-related marketing means linking a promotion to a good cause. One of the best-known examples is Tesco's Computers for Schools promotion. This has run every year since 1992: for a period of ten weeks, Tesco stores give a voucher to each customer for every £10 spent in-store. The vouchers can be redeemed by local schools against computer equipment—at the time of writing, over £100 million worth of computers had been supplied.

The promotion serves a number of functions. First, it attracts new customers into Tesco: even if they only stay for the period of the promotion, this represents a substantial chunk of business at a quiet time of year. Second, it is good for community relations—because people give the vouchers to their local school (usually of course their own children's school), Tesco acquires a human, local face. This is no mean feat for a giant multinational chain. Third, customers enjoy the warm glow of giving when they hand over the vouchers, even though the vouchers actually cost them nothing. Finally, Tesco is helping to ensure that the next generation of employees are not only computer literate, but also think well of Tesco.

In practice

- Find a local cause to link with, or set up your promotion in such a way that people can find a local cause for themselves.

- Be specific—offering to pay to some vague or unknown charity does not carry much weight.

- Allow your customers to get the warm glow of giving.

- Time-limit the promotion—otherwise it loses its impact, since it just becomes part of what people expect from you.

95 SET A SPRAT TO CATCH A MACKEREL

Loss leaders are a well-known ploy in retailing. Essentially, the store sells some popular item at a much-reduced price to attract people into the store, on the assumption that they are almost certain to buy something else as well. The profit comes from the "something elses." Fast-food restaurants often do the same thing, offering (say) two pizzas for the price of one on the assumption that customers will buy a bottle of wine, a dessert, a salad, or whatever.

Translating this into other business contexts may be another story, of course.

The idea

When voice-over-internet protocol (VOIP) was first developed it was difficult to see how to make money out of it. The free communications and information sharing capability of the internet was, until then, paid for from advertising, but it was hard to see how this could apply to voice communications. After all, no one would want their telephone conversations to be interrupted by advertising.

When Skype first started trading, the company decided to give away the Skype-to-Skype part of the business, so that members (not subscribers) could talk to each other indefinitely for nothing. This meant that people could call anywhere in the world to another Skype user, for as long as they wanted, without paying anything at all.

This was, of course, a very real advantage to a great many people. Skype conference calls could be arranged globally, at zero cost, and the system very quickly acquired over 12 million members. However,

Skype does not allow members to call landlines or cellphones free. These require a further (very modest) subscription, and that of course is where the money comes in. The cost of running the system is minimal—unlike other online businesses, there are no goods to send out or invoices to prepare, and people are simply billed by direct debit every time the subscription or the usage charges fall due.

Giving away something of real benefit has certainly benefited the founders of Skype: the company was sold to eBay for $2.6 billion in 2005.

In practice

- Ensure that what you give away has real value.

- The giveaway should not be sufficient in itself—there needs to be a strong potential for follow-up sales.

- If possible, the giveaway should encourage other people to join in with the scheme.

CONSIDER THE CULTURE

WE ARE ALWAYS being told that we live in a multicultural society, yet most of us know relatively little about the other cultures we deal with. This is a particularly acute problem when we are dealing over the telephone, since it requires our telephone staff (sometimes an entire call center full of them) to be culturally sensitive in many different ways to many different cultures.

The problem is exacerbated further by the fact that call centers often have a high staff turnover rate: these are jobs that are stressful, so there is a constant pressure to leave. Making cultural gaffes and annoying the customers simply adds to the stress.

The idea

Aviva is a major financial services player, and consequently the company runs several large call centers. In common with many other companies, Aviva has located some of its call centers in India, where costs are dramatically lower and an educated, English-speaking workforce is readily available. However, the vast majority of this workforce have never been to Britain, and are unlikely ever to do so, so Aviva runs courses on cultural understanding. The courses are not only about what people say, but how they say it: the courses cover issues such as the weather, the state of the roads, current issues in British politics, polite expressions and over-familiar or impolite expressions, and so forth.

The aim is not to allow call center operators to pretend that they are actually British: it is simply to ensure effective communication between call center staff and customers.

In practice

- Identify the cultural groups you might encounter.

- Take advice from a member of the target group—don't rely on your own judgments or published "cultural guides."

- Keep the training going—cultures shift, and anyway there is always more to learn.

BUILD A NEW DISTRIBUTION CHANNEL

Sometimes distribution channels are so tied up by existing companies it is difficult (even impossible) to get a product to market. Even when retailers can be identified, often part of the chain is contracted to some major supplier who blocks the distribution at the wholesale stage.

For small companies in particular, finding a route to market can present a major challenge: often the big boys are not interested unless there is a fairly substantial financial commitment in terms of renting shelf space or supplying large amounts of product on extended credit.

The idea

When Red Bull was first launched in Britain, it was an attempt to create the energy drinks market from scratch. The company was founded in Austria in 1984, but only started selling the drink in 1987.

Breaking into the British market proved difficult. The company wanted to target a young audience, partly because they would have the longest usage life and partly because young people often participate in sports or need to stay up late, either to party or to study. Red Bull therefore began by recruiting students to act as part-time salespeople, visiting nightclubs and sports centers to promote the drink. Since the nightclub owners were seeking to attract a young audience, the student salespeople represented a powerful influence.

Eventually Red Bull established its own warehousing and distribution, but again ran these using students as part-time workers. Apart from keeping costs down, this ensured that the entire workforce matched the brand values, and (perhaps even more importantly) were able to act as influencers, telling their friends about the product.

Today, Red Bull has reached the point where it sells 3 billion cans of the drink a year.

In practice

- Decide where you really want to sell your product, and focus on just those outlets.

- Decide who would be your best advocates for the product in those outlets.

- Follow up with a continued commitment to the distribution chain, even when other channels open up.

USE A WEBLOG

98

The internet has certainly fired people's imaginations, but the possibilities are far from being fully explored. At first, the internet was seen mainly as a kind of extension of traditional advertising— most websites were just presence sites, directing people to telephone or call into an office. The interactive possibilities were largely ignored.

However, it is the possibility of online interactions that makes the internet different from anything that has gone before. Consumers have been quick to flock to online forums and weblogs to express their opinions of companies and brands, yet companies have done relatively little to encourage or influence this.

The idea

When Toyota launched the new Auris in Greece, they identified a number of regular bloggers (weblog contributors) and gave them each a car to test drive for a week. Needless to say, they posted the results of the test drives on their blogs.

This fitted well with Toyota's desire to approach a young, affluent market: internet use in Greece is still less than in most European countries, and therefore the Greek internet system is dominated by better-off, educated, usually young people. Getting several reviews of the car onto blogs was a major coup for Toyota: there were 52,000 visits to the websites by 41,000 visitors, leading to over 2,000 requests for test drives.

In practice

- This is a risky strategy: if the bloggers don't like the product, you will have a lot of negative publicity to contend with.

- Make sure you identify the influential bloggers correctly.

- Give yourself the best chance of a successful outcome by making sure that the product samples they are given are absolutely perfect.

99 MAKE BUYING EASY

THE EASIER IT is to buy from you, the more likely people are to do it, and yet many firms put barriers in the way of their customers. For example, telephoning to order a takeaway meal to be delivered takes time and effort, not to mention telephone charges. People who order takeaway meals are either very tired or very lazy—the less effort they have to put in, the better.

The idea

Pizza Magic is a pizza delivery company based in Glasgow. The company delivers throughout the area, and of course most of the orders come in by telephone. Recently, however, the company hit on the idea of allowing customers to order pizzas online.

The company's website now has the menu, including of course the requisite wide range of additional toppings, and is interactive so that people can order the pizza of their choice and pay for it without speaking to a human being at all.

This has several advantages. First, people who are tired often do not want to talk to anybody, so ordering online is less hassle. Second, the company can easily change its menus, prices, topping options, and so forth without having to reprint all the menus. Third, automating the ordering process means less staff time spent on the telephone. Finally, the possibility of error in transcribing customer orders is virtually eliminated—any errors are likely to be on the customer's part, or possibly the chef's.

Of course, people can still order by telephone, or even call in—but the internet offers a very convenient option.

In practice

- Make the website as interactive and user-friendly as possible.

- Ensure that people can still order in the conventional way.

- Store all orders in case of disputes—if possible, send them to delivery personnel cellphones.

100 MAKE YOUR PRODUCT EASIER TO USE THAN EVERYBODY ELSE'S

THE EASIER IT is to use a product, the more likely it is that people will use and recommend it. Making products easy to use is sometimes not obvious—many technical people and engineers forget that most of us have little or no idea about the technical aspects of the products we use. Computer software is a fine example—most software is extremely difficult to learn, and appears to become more complex with every new edition.

That said, even the most simple day-to-day products can be made easier to use—and this often means that a whole new USP can be developed.

The idea

The British market for women's magazines is seriously crowded. Several hundred magazines compete for the attention of Britain's 20 million women, so launching a new one is extremely difficult.

Glamour is a magazine aimed at the 20-something career woman. This is a market that has been dominated by *Cosmopolitan* for the past 40 years, and is also the market that is most attractive to magazine publishers, so *Glamour* would have a real problem breaking in, if all its publishers did was produce a *Cosmo* clone.

Glamour is published in an unusual format, however. It has been made handbag-sized. This means that it is easy to carry around and read on crowded Tube trains or buses, while sitting in the hairdresser's, or even while walking. The magazine's content is nothing unusual—celebrity gossip, health and diet advice, and beauty tips—but the format is unique.

Fitting the product to the customer's needs has certainly paid off for *Glamour*.

In practice

- Observe people using your product. What difficulties do they experience?

- Work out ways to overcome the difficulties.

- Always test any changes in your product by showing them to real customers.